15 minute focus
Brief Counseling
Techniques that Work

SCHOOL-BASED CRISIS RESPONSE

UNDERSTANDING, PREPARING FOR, AND RECOVERING FROM CRISIS EVENTS

NATIONAL CENTER for
YOUTH ISSUES

Funding to help underwrite the development of
the *15-Minute Focus* series has been generously provided by:

PASTORAL INSTITUTE

SARAH T. BUTLER
CHILDREN'S CENTER
COLUMBUS, GEORGIA

The Sarah T. Butler Children's Center at the Pastoral Institute of
Columbus, Georgia is dedicated to the mental health and well-being
of children ages 1-18. This center provides comprehensive services
that span psychological testing, intervention, therapy groups, and
counseling. In all our activities we seek to inspire growth through faith,
hope, and love.

Duplication and Copyright

NCYI titles may be purchased in bulk at special discounts for
educational, business, fundraising, or promotional use.
For more information, please email sales@ncyi.org.

★
NATIONAL CENTER for
YOUTH ISSUES

P.O. Box 22185
Chattanooga, TN 37422-2185
423.899.5714 • 866.318.6294
fax: 423.899.4547 • www.ncyi.org

Print: 9781965066072
eBook: 9781965066089

The Library of Congress Control Number has been applied
for and can be obtained with the Library of Congress.

© 2025 National Center for Youth Issues, Chattanooga, TN
All rights reserved.
Written by: Michelle Sircy
Published by National Center for Youth Issues
Printed in the U.S.A. • February 2025

Dedication

To the schools, families, and communities that have walked through the storm of crisis together—your resilience, courage, and unwavering hope are a testament to the strength found in unity.

To the professionals who stood in the gap, offering comfort and unwavering support, holding space for healing, restoring hope, and reminding us all that even in our darkest moments, we are never alone. This book is for you.

Disclaimer

This book is not a replacement for comprehensive prevention training. It is designed to supplement such training and serve as a quick reference guide for school communities when they experience crisis events. While this guide provides valuable information and strategies for responding to crises, it is essential to undergo proper prevention and preparedness training through certified programs. Use this guide as a supplemental resource to enhance—not replace—formal training. The resource section of this guide includes training programs schools can consider.

It's also important for me to acknowledge the significant impact that my crisis-response training has had on my professional life and on how I approach managing crises. Over the course of leading responses to over 450 school-based crises, I've consistently drawn on my training in the **PREPaRE model.**[1] PREPaRE stands for:

- **P**revent and prepare for psychological trauma
- **R**eaffirm physical health and perceptions of safety and security
- **E**valuate psychological trauma risk
- **P**rovide interventions
- **a**nd
- **R**espond to psychological needs
- **E**xamine the effectiveness of crisis prevention and intervention

While the PREPaRE model heavily influenced my experience and approach, this guide is not strictly based on the PREPaRE model. Instead, it offers a broader framework that draws from various experiences and strategies in crisis response. If you're interested in learning more about the PREPaRE model and how to get training, please see the resource section at the back of this book.

Contents

**See page 113 for information about
Downloadable Resources and Templates**

Introduction

In today's educational landscape, effective crisis response in schools is more crucial than ever. Schools are meant to be safe havens for students, but unfortunately, crises—ranging from natural disasters to acts of violence—can and do occur. How a school community responds to these events can significantly affect the recovery and well-being of its students, staff, and families.

I have led over 450 school-based crisis response events as a district crisis lead in a large urban school district. I recall many situations where a quick reference guide would have been invaluable. Amid the initial shock and chaos of a crisis, the urgent need for a well-structured, organized, and swift response can be overwhelming, often making it difficult to recall one's training. In those moments, accessible, practical resources can guide school leaders through the development of comprehensive crisis support. The need for this type of resource drove my commitment to develop a guide that serves as a lifeline for school and district leaders during challenging times.

This guide is structured to provide clear, actionable steps for school crisis response. It is divided into several sections:

- Preparation and Prevention
- Immediate Response
- Recovery
- Long-term Support

Each section includes detailed checklists, practical tips, and case studies to illustrate effective strategies and common pitfalls. The purpose of this guide is to empower school communities with the knowledge and tools they need to navigate the aftermath of a crisis, ensuring that every member of the school community receives the support they need.

This guide offers a reliable companion for those difficult moments when quick, thoughtful, and effective action is needed the most.

1 Understanding School Crises

Scenario: Severe Weather

Imagine a typical school day suddenly disrupted by a severe weather alert. The skies darken, and a tornado warning is issued. Teachers quickly usher students to designated safe areas while the administration coordinates with emergency services. Thankfully, the school is not hit by the tornado, but a neighborhood where several of your students and staff live is affected. Students start to share images of the damage on social media. Worry and chaos quickly erupt.

Schools must be prepared to handle a wide variety of crises that can impact them directly or indirectly. Since schools are direct reflections of the communities they serve, school and district leaders must be able to respond quickly and efficiently to a multitude of situations. To be able to respond to everything from natural disasters and student or staff deaths to community violence and bus accidents is a tall order for school and district leaders. Although comprehensive training and planning may, and should, be in place, it can be a challenge in the midst of a crisis to recall exactly what should take place to serve the students, staff, and families we serve.

Before we can start talking about strategies for addressing crisis events, we must understand the different types of crises that school leaders may face. While it's impossible to create an exhaustive list of potential crises—new situations can arise daily (consider the unforeseen global pandemic)—we can focus on the most common ones. This knowledge not only helps us prepare for anticipated situations but also equips us to better handle unexpected events. **By learning about the typical crises schools encounter, we can build a foundation that enhances our ability to respond effectively to the unknown.**

Let's consider the scenario above. Schools regularly conduct tornado drills, ensuring that students and staff know how to move quickly to take cover and prepare for tornadoes or other natural disasters. However, the critical question is: do school leaders and staff know what to do if a tornado strikes the school or the surrounding community? Are they equipped to activate the school or district crisis-response plan (i.e., the emergency operations plan, EOP) and address student needs until additional support arrives? From my experience, while schools are proficient in taking shelter, practice and training for the steps that follow— those that are crucial for effective crisis management and support—are often inadequate. This gap highlights the need for comprehensive crisis-response training that goes beyond initial emergency procedures.

Types of School Crises

It's impossible to create an exhaustive list of the types of crises a school can face. However, in this section, we will examine the most common ones. By exploring various crisis events that may affect schools, we can better prepare for unforeseen. We will examine the following categories: Natural Disasters, Violence, Accidents, Health Emergencies, and Community Crises.

Natural Disasters

- **Tornadoes:** Sudden, severe weather events causing extensive damage and posing significant risks to student and staff safety.
- **Earthquakes:** Unpredictable natural events causing structural damage and potential injuries.
- **Floods:** Water-related disasters affecting school infrastructure and accessibility.

- **Hurricanes:** Large-scale weather events with extensive warning, but severe potential damage and disruption.
- **Wildfires:** Large, destructive fires that spread quickly.
- **Blizzards:** Severe snowstorms with high winds and low visibility.

Violence

- **School Shootings:** Tragically, these have become more frequent, requiring immediate lockdown and reunification procedures, as well as long-term emotional support.
- **Physical Fights:** Conflicts between students or between students and staff, needing de-escalation and conflict resolution.
- **Assaults:** Incidents of physical or sexual violence requiring immediate intervention and support services.
- **Racism:** Discrimination, prejudice, or bias based on race or ethnicity, which can manifest in various forms, such as verbal abuse, physical violence, exclusion, or systemic inequalities.
- **Hate Crimes:** Criminal acts motivated by bias or prejudice toward a particular group based on race, religion, sexual orientation, ethnicity, gender, or other characteristics.
- **Swatting:** False reports made to emergency services, often resulting in a heavy police response to a non-existent threat, causing disruption, fear, and potential harm to the school community.

Accidents

- **Bus Crashes:** Incidents during school transportation requiring immediate medical response and coordination with families.
- **Student/Staff Hit by a Vehicle:** Accidents in which a student or staff member is struck by a vehicle with or without injury.
- **Student/Staff Involved in Car Accident:** Car accidents in which a student or staff member was involved, with an injury reported.
- **Playground Injuries:** Common yet serious accidents occurring during recess or physical education.
- **Fire:** Fire that is either naturally caused, or intentionally set, to the school building or campus.

Health/Mental Health Emergencies

- **Infectious Disease Outbreaks:** Situations like flu epidemics or, more recently, COVID-19, requiring comprehensive health measures and possible school closures.
- **Student or Staff Medical Emergencies:** Sudden health crises like heart attacks, severe allergic reactions, or asthma attacks requiring quick medical response.
- **Student or Staff with Terminal Illness:** A member of the school family has been diagnosed with a terminal illness.
- **Mental Health Emergency (Student or Staff):** A mental health crisis that requires intervention from a mental health professional.
- **Non-Suicidal Self-Injurious Harm:** Incidents where a student or staff member engages in self-harm without suicidal intent.
- **Student or Staff Suicide:** A member of the school family has died by suicide.

Community Crises

- **Community Violence:** Incidents of violence in the community, which impact students and staff emotionally and sometimes physically.
- **Nearby Industrial Accidents:** Events such as chemical spills or explosions in nearby industrial areas affecting the school environment.
- **Acts of Hate and Violence:** Acts of hate and violence may be associated with a person's race, gender, sex, sexual orientation, religious practices, or gang affiliation. It may also be random but it has caused fear within the community.

Five Mission Areas of Crisis Preparedness

Schools face a wide range of potential emergencies, from natural disasters and accidents to acts of violence and public health crises. Effective crisis preparedness requires a comprehensive approach that addresses every stage of an emergency, from prevention to recovery. According to FEMA, the Five Mission Areas of Crisis Preparedness—Prevention, Protection, Mitigation, Response, and Recovery—offer a structured framework to guide schools in building resilience and ensuring the safety of their students, staff, and communities.[2]

The Five Mission Areas of Crisis Preparedness provide a structured approach to emergency management, as outlined by the Federal Emergency Management Agency (FEMA). These mission areas are integral to frameworks such as the PREPaRE model and the Guide for Developing High-Quality School Emergency Operations Plans (EOPs), aligning with standards set by the US Departments of Education, Homeland Security, and FEMA.

- **Prevention** involves proactive steps like establishing social-emotional learning programs to build a positive school culture or conducting routine safety audits to identify potential risks.
- **Protection** focuses on safeguarding students and staff through measures like implementing secure entry systems or maintaining up-to-date emergency contact protocols. Together, these actions reduce the likelihood of emergencies and enhance the school's overall preparedness.
- **Mitigation** involves minimizing the potential effects of crises by creating detailed evacuation plans or securing hazardous materials on campus.
- **Response** ensures swift action during an emergency, such as coordinating with first responders or activating reunification processes for families.
- **Recovery** helps the school community rebuild and heal, incorporating strategies like providing trauma-informed support for students and conducting post-incident evaluations to improve future preparedness.

By embracing the Five Mission Areas—Prevention, Protection, Mitigation, Response, and Recovery—schools can create a cohesive and proactive approach to crisis preparedness. These mission areas are not stand-alone steps but interconnected parts of a continuous process aimed at fostering safety, resilience, and recovery. We will discuss these themes throughout the book.

Impact of Crises on Students, Staff, and the School Community

Every person is impacted by crises differently based on their own traumatic experiences, coping skills, current mental health, and personal support system. With this in mind, school leaders must plan a tiered system of support that will meet the varied needs of the school community. Tiered systems for crisis support follow the structure of other school-wide support models such as Positive Behavior Intervention and Support (PBIS) or Multi-Tiered Systems of Support (MTSS).

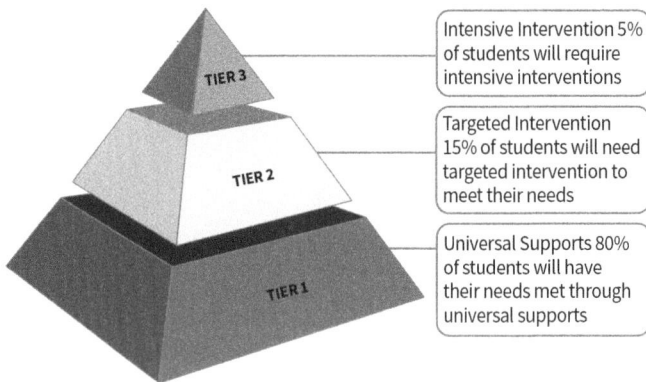

TIER 3 — Intensive Intervention 5% of students will require intensive interventions

TIER 2 — Targeted Intervention 15% of students will need targeted intervention to meet their needs

TIER 1 — Universal Supports 80% of students will have their needs met through universal supports

Tier 1 (Universal)

Tier 1 (Universal) meets the needs of 80–90 percent of the school community by providing interventions that everyone receives. Examples of Tier 1 crisis support include whole-class instruction, teaching students coping strategies, and leading mindfulness exercises. School leaders and school-based mental health professionals will also triage student needs at this level and make referrals for Tier 2 services as necessary. The primary focus is on creating an environment where students feel cared for and have a strong sense of belonging and safety.

Tier 2 (Targeted Intervention)

Tier 2 (Targeted Intervention) meets the needs of 5–15 percent of the school community through short-term interventions for targeted groups identified based on data. Examples of Tier 2 crisis support include strength-based small-group counseling, brief individual counseling, and conducting risk assessments. The primary focus is on early intervention to promote mental health and well-being, while also identifying students who may need more intensive, long-term support and making appropriate referrals for Tier 3 services.

Tier 3 (Intensive Intervention)

Tier 3 (Intensive Intervention) meets the needs of 1–5 percent of the school community. This level provides targeted referrals and services for individuals with intensive health needs requiring intensive support and follow-up. Based on the data, long-term interventions are needed for a targeted group of people impacted. Examples of Tier 3 crisis support include long-term therapeutic counseling and outpatient or inpatient treatment.

We will use the tiered support model throughout this book to examine intervention levels that may benefit the school community. The most important factor that school leaders need to be mindful of is that there is not a "one-size-fits-all" approach to school crisis response. Each school should use a cross-disciplinary professional team to closely examine resources that can be used within the school and the community during times of crisis.

It is important to highlight that, immediately following a crisis event, individuals are not ready to process their feelings or emotions. **There is a distinct difference between counseling services (provided over time with the goal of problem resolution) versus crisis-intervention services (provided in the short term with the goal of helping the individual and community take steps toward adaptive coping).** Some individuals may need more formal counseling services following exposure to a traumatic event, and for others the crisis-intervention services paired with social supports will be enough.

While school leaders and school-based mental health professionals may want to initiate counseling services immediately following a crisis event, those impacted are not psychologically ready to process their feelings and emotions in the immediate aftermath of a crisis. The primary goal in the immediate aftermath of crisis exposure is to provide crisis-intervention services that create an environment in which students and staff feel safe and understand basic strategies to manage anxiety and grief. Such services should also ensure effective triaging so those needing long-term support are identified and referred for appropriate mental health services. Formal counseling services are only recommended for those whose needs exceed what the crisis-intervention services can provide.

Importance of a Coordinated Crisis-Response Plan

A well-structured crisis plan provides a clear framework for responding to various types of emergencies, enabling school leaders and staff to act quickly and effectively. When I train new school counselors or teach counselor preparation courses, crisis response is the number one source of anxiety for them. Other school and district leaders share the same concern about school-based crisis preparedness and the intense desire to respond effectively without causing additional harm to their communities.

Having a coordinated crisis-response plan created by a comprehensive cross-disciplinary team alleviates the burden on individual school leaders. It allows a group of professionals to collaboratively develop a plan that will guide the school during a crisis. Let's examine a few of the benefits of having a coordinated response plan.

Ensures Rapid Response

A coordinated crisis plan enables swift and organized action, reducing chaos and confusion during an emergency. This rapid response can significantly mitigate the impact of the crisis on students, staff, and the broader community.

Defines Roles and Responsibilities

Clearly outlined roles and responsibilities ensure that everyone knows what to do during a crisis. This clarity helps responders prevent overlap, omissions, and delays and handle critical tasks promptly and efficiently.

Promotes Consistent Communication

Effective communication is vital during a crisis. A coordinated plan includes established communication protocols for disseminating information to students, staff, families, and the media, ensuring accurate and timely updates.

Provides Comprehensive Support

A crisis plan encompasses a tiered structure of support. This approach ensures that all members of the school community receive the appropriate level of care and support, tailored to their specific needs.

Facilitates Collaboration

A coordinated crisis plan fosters collaboration between school personnel, mental health professionals, emergency responders, state and federal response agencies, and community organizations. This teamwork enhances the overall response and ensures that responders utilize a wide range of resources and expertise.

Addresses Legal and Ethical Considerations

Adhering to legal and ethical standards is crucial during a crisis. A well-developed plan ensures compliance with relevant laws and regulations, such as reporting requirements and confidentiality protections, safeguarding the rights and well-being of all involved.

Enhances Preparedness and Resilience

Regularly practicing and updating the crisis plan helps build a culture of preparedness and resilience within the school community. This proactive approach equips individuals with the skills and confidence needed to handle crises effectively.

Supports Recovery and Continuous Improvement:

A comprehensive crisis plan includes strategies for post-crisis recovery and continuous improvement. By evaluating the response to each crisis, schools can identify lessons learned and make necessary adjustments to improve future preparedness.

Think back to the scenario at the beginning of this chapter. If the school leaders had a plan not only for warning drills but also for how the school would respond in the event of a natural disaster, they would have been better equipped to address the needs of the school community immediately. Key partners within the community would have been identified, tiered support structures would have been established, and each member of the school would have known their role in the response.

Developing a support plan during a crisis, when emotions are high, is not ideal. It's difficult to think systematically through all the components of a thorough and effective support system under such pressure. A coordinated crisis plan guides a structured and efficient response, promotes safety and well-being, and supports the recovery and resilience of the entire school community.

Legal and Ethical Considerations in Crisis Response

Legal and ethical considerations are vital in any crisis response, guiding the actions of school leaders and staff to ensure the safety, well-being, and rights of all individuals involved. Each school district should have policies and procedures that schools must follow in the event of a crisis. However, there are additional, broader areas of concern that should be considered as well. We will explore a few of those here.

Confidentiality is always at the forefront of the minds of school leaders. Schools must adhere to laws such as the **Family Educational Rights and Privacy Act (FERPA)** and, at times, the **Health Insurance Portability and Accountability Act (HIPAA)** when handling confidential student and staff information. Respecting individuals' privacy and confidentiality is essential for building trust and maintaining ethical standards. Even during times of crisis, school leaders must ensure they are closely adhering to confidentiality practices and protecting student information. This is a point of consideration when outside agencies are utilized during a crisis response.

Under FERPA, schools can share student information without permission during emergencies to keep people safe from immediate threats. These disclosures should only happen while the emergency is ongoing, be shared with those who need the information (like law enforcement or health officials), and be properly recorded with details about the situation. This exception is meant for urgent situations where quick action is needed. Schools should carefully decide if sharing the information is truly necessary and appropriate. For more information about the FERPA emergency exception, school leaders can visit their website. [3]

In addition to confidentiality, schools also have a duty to care, meaning they have a legal duty to provide a safe and secure environment for students and staff. Failure to do so may result in legal liability. For example, schools operate in loco parentis, a Latin phrase that means "in the place of a parent." This grants schools certain parental rights, responsibilities, and authority to act in the best interests of the students while they are under the school's care.

Under *in loco parentis*, schools are required to implement measures that protect students' physical and emotional safety. This involves creating a nurturing environment that supports the student's ability to learn and thrive within the school setting. This duty becomes even more prominent in times of crisis as schools must rapidly adapt to protect and support their students. The obligation extends to ensuring that comprehensive crisis-response plans are in place that are proactive, thorough, and sensitive to the needs of all students, recognizing that each student's needs may vary significantly based on their personal experiences and existing vulnerabilities.

Last, an essential element of any crisis-response plan is the fair and equitable allocation of resources. Schools must ensure that all individuals receive the support they need during a crisis response, using resources effectively and efficiently to maximize support for those in need. Additionally, school leaders must ensure that their crisis-response efforts are culturally sensitive and inclusive, complying with laws such as **Title VI of the Civil Rights Act** and the **Individuals with Disabilities Education Act (IDEA)**. Recognizing and respecting cultural differences and diversity is crucial for providing equitable and effective crisis support. When developing the crisis-response plan, the team should be mindful of varying cultural differences that exist within the school, especially around death, burial rituals, and views on mental health.

For school leaders interested in researching **court cases involving schools**, several reliable sources can provide detailed case information, legal analyses, outcomes, and implications.

- **FindLaw** provides free access to a wide selection of case law and statutes. It includes a section specifically dedicated to education law, which covers various issues related to schools.[4]
  https://www.findlaw.com

- **Justia** offers free access to federal and state court decisions, including those involving school districts and educational issues. It is a useful tool for preliminary legal research.[5]
  https://www.justia.com

- **National School Boards Association (NSBA)** provides resources and publications discussing significant legal cases involving education policy and school administration. This resource helps leaders to understand the broader implications of legal decisions on schools.[6]
  https://www.nsba.org

- **Education Law Association (ELA)** offers resources and publications on a range of legal issues affecting education. They also summarize key court cases and legal trends that impact school governance and policy.[7]
  https://www.educationlaw.org

WRAP-UP

Schools must be prepared to handle a wide array of crises, reflecting the diverse challenges faced by the communities they serve. These crises can range from natural disasters, such as tornadoes and earthquakes, to incidents of violence, including school shootings and physical assaults. Accidents, health emergencies, and community crises further complicate the landscape of potential impactful occurrences. Understanding these **common types of crises** is essential for school leaders, as it enables them to build a foundation for effective response strategies and better manage unexpected events.

School responders require a **comprehensive crisis-response plan** to ensure the safety and well-being of students, staff, and the broader school community. This plan should include a tiered support system, similar to Positive Behavior Intervention and Support (PBIS) or Multi-Tiered Systems of Support (MTSS), to address the varying needs of individuals affected by a crisis. Tier 1 interventions provide universal support, Tier 2 offers targeted help for those needing more focused assistance, and Tier 3 delivers intensive support and referral for trauma-informed therapeutic supports for those with the most severe needs. Such a model ensures that the school community receives appropriate care and support during and after a crisis.

Legal and ethical considerations are critical components of any crisis-response plan. Schools must adhere to laws such as the Family Educational Rights and Privacy Act (FERPA) and at times the Health Insurance Portability and Accountability Act (HIPAA) to protect the confidentiality and privacy of students and staff. Additionally, school leaders have a duty of care to provide a safe environment and must ensure equitable resource allocation and culturally sensitive support. Schools can create a structured and efficient approach to responding to crises, promoting safety, and fostering resilience within their communities by developing a coordinated crisis-response plan that addresses these legal and ethical issues.

QUESTIONS to CONSIDER

1. Does your school's crisis-response plan include response protocols to address a variety of crisis situations?

2. Does your school/district engage a multidisciplinary team to plan and prepare for a crisis response should a situation impact your school? If not, who on your staff could you collaborate with to develop a multidisciplinary team to create a tiered-support model?

3. Do you currently have a support structure in place to meet your students' and staff's emotional, mental, and physical health needs?

4. How can schools ensure that their crisis-response efforts are equitable and culturally sensitive?

5. What steps can leaders take to ensure that all school staff are adequately trained and confident in their roles during a crisis vs. simply knowing how to run a proper drill?

2 Preparing for a Crisis

Scenario: School Bus Accident

A school bus carrying thirty middle school students was involved in a severe accident with a semi-truck on the way to school. Several students and the bus driver sustained injuries, and emergency services have begun transporting students to the local hospital. This is the last day of school before winter break, and you are already short on staff, but you know you need to have a presence at the hospital and the accident site. To complicate things, students are receiving pictures and details about the accident through social media, leading to panic and distress within your student body.

Crisis response involves thorough planning in advance but also requires the flexibility to adapt quickly to diverse situations and staffing challenges. The scenario described is a common occurrence that school leaders must navigate. Even with the most comprehensive crisis plans, we must make real-time adjustments based on the specifics of the incident. Effective crisis management demands clear communication, swift decision-making, and the ability to mobilize resources efficiently. Easy to do, right?

To manage all the difficulties and complexities of a comprehensive crisis response, leaders must compile a school-based crisis-response team. Many districts, educational cooperatives, or state education departments have larger teams that can assist and support the school team in situations that have a large-scale impact on the school community. However, school leaders need a school-based team that knows the school and can guide larger response efforts if/when needed. Having a dedicated school-based crisis team who knows the school community helps ensure that immediate and knowledgeable action can be taken to support the school community effectively, even if a larger team needs to assist.

In this chapter, we will look at ways to prepare for crises that impact the school community. Continuous training, evaluation, and improvement of our crisis-response strategies are essential to handle any unforeseen circumstances effectively. It is impossible to prepare for every scenario that could occur, but we can develop a flexible plan that allows us to adapt and pivot in our responses when needed.

School Based Crisis-Response Team: What Is It and Who Is on It?

A school-based crisis team is a compilation of professionals who work at a school and participate in training on preparedness and response specifically in a school setting. They work collaboratively with district and community resources to quickly and effectively meet the needs of students, staff, and families. The team's primary goal is to ensure the safety, well-being, and mental health of everyone involved with a goal to return to a normal routine as quickly as possible. The team also triages students and staff to identify those who need more intensive interventions and follow up with appropriate referrals.

In addition to their immediate response efforts, the school-based crisis response team plays an important role in prevention and education. They can implement training and workshops aimed at building resilience and awareness among students and staff. The team can also conduct drills and update emergency protocols to ensure the school is always prepared for unexpected events. By fostering a supportive and proactive environment, the crisis team not only addresses crises as they occur but also strengthens the overall safety and well-being of the school community. This comprehensive approach ensures that everyone is equipped with the knowledge and resources needed to navigate challenging situations, promoting a culture of readiness and care.

.Managing a school crisis requires a delicate balance of empathy, quick thinking, and coordinated action. Each member of the crisis team must be adept at handling high-pressure situations while maintaining clear and calm communication. The team often works behind the scenes, planning and preparing for various scenarios, ensuring that they can respond swiftly and effectively when a crisis does arise. They should also stay updated on best practices and new strategies in crisis management, participating in ongoing training and professional development. Their preparedness is what makes a significant difference in mitigating the impact of crises on the school community.

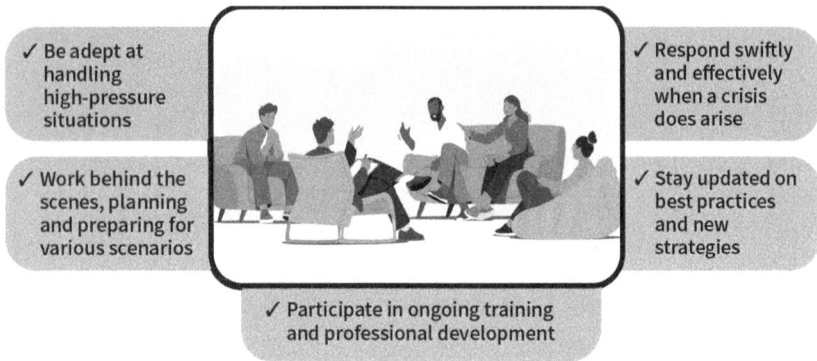

- ✓ Be adept at handling high-pressure situations
- ✓ Respond swiftly and effectively when a crisis does arise
- ✓ Work behind the scenes, planning and preparing for various scenarios
- ✓ Stay updated on best practices and new strategies
- ✓ Participate in ongoing training and professional development

Now that we know what a school-based crisis respone team is, let's explore who can make up your school-based team. When we are developing our team, we want to look at professionals who work in the school. These individuals know your school, students, staff, schedule, and the intricacies that make your school unique. The people on your team are people whom your students and staff have seen, and, in an ideal world, with whom they already have relationships. School leaders should aim to include a diverse group of professionals with different backgrounds and training to provide a well-rounded perspective for the team.

Potential Members of a School-Based Crisis Response Team

Principal

The principal plays an active role in the school-based crisis response team. They have the final say in decisions and communicate with district administration and external agencies. The principal also makes the final decision on who will be on the crisis team and assigns roles and responsibilities. They do, however, rely heavily on the expertise of the other professionals on the team. They may also lead the crisis response but must always have a designee in case they are unavailable to lead the response or it is best for their designee to lead the response.

Assistant Principal

The assistant principal's primary responsibility is to assist the principal with logistics or other specific tasks assigned by the principal. The assistant principal may also help with scheduling drills and ensuring that everyone knows how to respond in emergencies. They help support the logistic needs of the crisis response.

School Counselor

Oftentimes, given their training in mental health and crisis response, the school counselor will take a leadership role on the crisis team. They will give advice and guide the principal and other members of the team on the needs of the students and staff. They provide immediate crisis-intervention support to students and staff, help manage stress and trauma responses, and coordinate with external mental health professionals.

School Psychologist

The school psychologist and school counselor work collaboratively together as experts in the social, emotional, and mental well-being of students and staff. The school psychologist can share the responsibilities of the school counselor, co-leading response services and guiding the principal (or designee) in decision-making.

School Social Worker

School social workers work collaboratively with the school counselor and school psychologist to meet the immediate needs of students and families impacted by the crisis. They also work with community resources and make referrals for ongoing services.

School Resource Officer

The school resource officer can act as a liaison between the school and local law enforcement. They provide security and safety and manage law enforcement-related issues.

Support Staff

School support staff play an important role in crisis response as they will work closely on logistics and distribution of information. They will assist in distributing supplies, securing space for response services, and the coordination of resources.

Depending on the professionals the school employs, **additional roles may be added**, or adjusted, to the crisis-response team based on their training and experience. These roles can enhance the team's capacity to manage and respond to crises effectively. For example, if a school has a special education or multilingual learner specialist, they would be invaluable members of the crisis-response team. They would also ensure that special needs are addressed within crisis preparedness and are incorporated into the crisis-response plan (see Safe and Sound Schools, *Especially Safe* curriculum[8]). The special education specialist would ensure that students with disabilities receive appropriate care and accommodations during a crisis, coordinating with other staff to develop individualized crisis plans (if needed) and providing necessary support.

Similarly, the multilingual learner specialist would facilitate communication with students and their families, ensuring that all stakeholders receive clear and accurate information in their native language. They would provide translation and interpretation services, helping to bridge language barriers and ensuring that everyone is informed and supported during and after the crisis. **These specialists' unique expertise enhances the team's ability to address diverse needs within the school community.**

Developing a Comprehensive Crisis-Response Plan

Risk Assessment

Developing a crisis-response plan involves a meticulous and collaborative approach to ensure comprehensive preparedness for various emergencies. The process begins with a risk assessment, identifying potential threats such as natural disasters, violent incidents, health emergencies, and other unforeseen events. This assessment should consider the specific vulnerabilities of the school, including its geographic location, infrastructure, and population demographics.

Emergency Procedures

Once potential risks are identified, the next step is to establish clear and detailed emergency procedures tailored to each scenario. These procedures should include protocols for lockdowns, evacuations, shelter-in-place orders, delivery of social/emotional/mental wellness, and a reunification process if needed. Each protocol should outline specific actions for students, staff, and emergency responders, ensuring everyone knows their roles and responsibilities. Later in this book, we will discuss specific crises and things to consider and plan for.

Communication

Effective communication is a cornerstone of a successful crisis-response plan. The plan should establish a robust communication strategy, including designated communication officers, clear messaging templates, and multiple channels (e.g., PA systems, emails, text alerts) to disseminate information rapidly. This strategy must ensure that timely and accurate information reaches all stakeholders, including students, staff, parents, emergency services, and the wider community.

Resource Allocation

Resource allocation is another critical component. The plan should specify the location and availability of essential resources such as first aid kits, emergency food and water supplies, medical equipment, and communication devices. It should also outline procedures for accessing additional resources during a crisis, including partnerships with local emergency services and community organizations.

Training and Drills

Regular training and drills are essential to reinforce the crisis-response plan. These activities should involve all members of the school-based crisis response team and include various scenarios that will require changes and alterations to the current crisis plan. Rarely will a crisis occur that does not require the team to make adjustments. Feedback from these drills should be used to refine and improve the plan continually.

Recovery Strategy

The plan should also include a comprehensive recovery strategy to address the aftermath of a crisis. This strategy should focus on the emotional and psychological well-being of students and staff, providing counseling services, support groups, and other resources to help them cope with trauma and stress. It should also outline the steps of the reunification process to make sure students are safely reunited with their caregivers. Unfortunately, the reunification process is often not planned for and can have long-lasting and negative impacts on the entire school community, causing additional trauma to all involved. *The I Love You Guys Foundation* offers comprehensive training in the reunification process for schools and districts.[9]

Evaulation and Updating

Continuous evaluation and updating of the crisis-response plan are vital to its long-term effectiveness. This involves regular reviews based on feedback from drills, actual incidents, and new information or changes in best practices. The crisis-response team should meet periodically to assess the plan's effectiveness and make necessary adjustments. It is especially important that, after a crisis occurs, the team meets to debrief on what went well and areas for improvement. We will discuss this more later in the book.

Planning for the Needs of Vulnerable or Unique Populations

Effective crisis-response planning must consider the diverse needs of all students, particularly those who are vulnerable or have unique needs. Earlier, we discussed special-needs students and multilingual learners, but schools have additional student populations with unique needs. For example, schools will have students who have medical needs or students who have specific emotional or behavioral needs. For teams to stay proactive in the care their students will require, this component should be reviewed at each meeting. As students enroll and unenroll, or as their needs evolve throughout the school year, continuous analysis and updates will be needed.

Some specific areas for school-based crisis response teams to consider when working with vulnerable or unique populations are:

Identification

- Regularly update the needs of students with disabilities, medical conditions, language barriers, and other unique needs.
- Maintain comprehensive records and ensure easy access for crisis team and staff members.
- Identify staff that may have unique needs (i.e., staff with preexisting medical conditions or concerns).

Individualized Planning

- Tailor emergency procedures to accommodate specific needs, including mobility, communication, and medical care.
- Provide translation services and multilingual communication materials for non-English speaking students and their families.
- Employ bilingual staff members to facilitate communication during emergencies or identify and practice using translation services available through apps and websites.
- Identify students who may require additional emotional and behavioral support during crises.

Medical Preparedness

- Keep an updated list of students with medical needs, including required medications and medical equipment.
- Train staff in administering medications and handling medical emergencies.

There may be additional needs your crisis team identifies as unique circumstances that require special planning. By continually assessing and addressing these unique circumstances, your crisis team can ensure that the school's emergency response plan remains comprehensive, inclusive, and capable of adapting to the evolving needs of all students.

Direct and Indirect Crisis

Crisis events can either directly impact the school community or have an indirect effect, even if they do not occur at the school or to students/staff that attend the school. Direct impact crises, such as natural disasters, school violence, or the death of a student or staff member, have an immediate and profound impact on the school community. These events require immediate response and support to ensure the safety and well-being of those directly affected.

However, other events can occur within the community, country, or world that also impact the school. These indirect crises might include community violence, wars or attacks on specific populations, widespread health epidemics, racism, or significant political and social unrest. Even though these events happen outside the school, they can create an atmosphere of fear, uncertainty, and stress, affecting students' and staff's mental and emotional health. Therefore, **schools should have comprehensive crisis-response plans that address both direct and indirect impacts to effectively support their communities through any crisis.**

Let's go back to our scenario from the beginning of this chapter. The school the students attended would be directly impacted by the bus accident. However, since we know students are texting and messaging their friends with graphic pictures from the accident, it is highly probable that students from other schools will also be heavily impacted. Social media complicates this situation as students can quickly share information through various platforms. This rapid dissemination of information can lead to widespread emotional distress, rumors, and misinformation, amplifying the crisis's impact beyond the immediate school community. Coordinated efforts between schools can help manage the broader implications of the crisis, ensuring that all students receive the care and support they need during such challenging times.

School-based crisis response teams need to be aware and proactive in keeping informed of both direct and indirect situations that are unfolding in our world that could impact our students. By staying mindful and vigilant, the crisis team can quickly address the immediate needs of students, thereby limiting the long-term impact these events may have. **This proactive approach involves monitoring local, national, and global news, maintaining open lines of communication with community organizations and emergency services, and regularly assessing the potential effects of external events on the school community.** By anticipating and preparing for these challenges, crisis teams can implement timely interventions, provide necessary support, and ensure the well-being and resilience of students and staff.

Establishing Partnerships with Community Resources

Community-based agencies are an integral part of a school-based crisis response team. When established correctly, they can become the heart of the -based team, complementing the work done during a crisis response and providing essential long-term care and family support. These agencies bring specialized expertise and resources that enhance the school's ability to address the diverse needs of students and staff in times of crisis. Mental health organizations, for instance, can offer immediate counseling and emotional support, helping individuals cope with trauma and stress, while also providing long-term therapeutic services to ensure ongoing recovery and resilience.

Additionally, community-based agencies can assist in addressing socioeconomic challenges that may arise during a crisis. They can provide essential resources such as food, clothing, housing assistance, and financial support to families in need, ensuring that the broader impacts of the crisis are mitigated. Doing so helps stabilize the home environment, allowing students and families to focus on their healing and well-being to reduce the negative impact of trauma as much as possible. These agencies play a significant role in creating a supportive network that addresses immediate needs and long-term recovery, fostering resilience and ensuring that students can continue their education and personal development without the added burden of unmet basic needs.

When the school-based crisis response team develops its crisis plans, evaluates its current capacity, and identifies resources within the community, it enhances services to students, staff, and families. Due to the vast differences between school funding, internal resources, and professional capacities, school-based crisis response teams should conduct a needs assessment and create a community resource map to help identify areas of need and possible community agencies available to meet those needs. Conducting a needs assessment allows the crisis team to understand the specific requirements of their school community, such as mental health support, emergency medical care, and food security. This assessment provides a clear picture of the gaps in current resources and highlights the areas where external support is indispensable.

Creating a community resource map based on the needs assessment helps the crisis team identify and organize local agencies and resources to provide necessary services during a crisis. This map serves as a visual tool, making it easy to see quickly which organizations can offer support and how to contact them in an emergency. By mapping out these resources, schools can ensure that they have a comprehensive network of support that can be mobilized effectively when needed.

After the principal has established who will serve on the crisis team and defined the roles they will play, the team should conduct a needs assessment followed by community resource mapping. This structured approach ensures that the team comprehensively understands the specific needs of the school community and the resources available to address those needs.

To assist in this process, the team can utilize the *School Mental Health Quality Guide Needs Assessment and Resource Mapping,* developed by the University of Maryland.[10] This guide provides a systematic approach to evaluating the current capacity of the school and identifying community resources that can enhance services to students, staff, and families.

Let's look back at the scenario from the beginning of this chapter. If schools are prepared and have already developed partnerships with community agencies, they could contact these partners to immediately provide support to students, especially on days when there is low staff availability. For example, one of the most impactful interventions during times of crisis is the use of animal-assisted crisis response. However, most schools do not have the insurance coverage, trained certified animals, or handlers to immediately implement this intervention. This is where community partners can step in and supplement the services the school can provide.

The importance of community partners cannot be overstated. A strong school-based crisis response team is aware of the unique needs of their school and which organizations can support those needs. These partnerships enable the school to tap into a broader range of services and resources, ensuring that students receive comprehensive care and support during a crisis. Community partners, such as local mental health agencies, non-profit organizations, and specialized service providers, can offer expertise and resources that the school may not possess internally.

WRAP-UP

In this chapter, we explored the critical components of **preparing for a crisis** within a school setting. Effective crisis response requires thorough planning and the flexibility to adapt quickly to diverse situations and staffing challenges. Real-time adjustments are often necessary based on the specifics of the incident, emphasizing the need for clear communication, swift decision-making, and efficient resource mobilization.

We delved into the formation and roles of a **school-based crisis response team**, which includes professionals such as the principal, assistant principal, school counselor, school psychologist, school social worker, school resource officer, safety and security personnel, and support staff. The team collaborates with district and community resources to meet the needs of students, staff, and families. Special attention must be given to planning for the needs of vulnerable or unique populations, such as students with disabilities, medical conditions, or language barriers. Regularly updating these needs and tailoring emergency procedures to accommodate specific requirements ensures the crisis-response plan remains comprehensive and inclusive.

We also discussed the impact of both **direct and indirect crisis events**. Direct crises occur within the school and require immediate response, while indirect crises, like community violence or war, can still affect the school. Effective crisis-response plans must address both. Establishing partnerships with **community-based agencies** enhances crisis response by providing specialized expertise and resources. Conducting a needs assessment and creating a community resource map can help identify and organize these resources for a well-coordinated response.

QUESTIONS to CONSIDER

1. Who will serve on our crisis-response team, and what roles will they play? Do you have backup personnel assigned?

2. How often will our team meet and what information will constitute standing agenda items for the team to cover?

3. What training and professional development opportunities will we provide for team members?

4. What vulnerable populations do we have at our school and what specific needs do we need to address?

5. Have we conducted a needs assessment to identify areas of need and resources?

6. Have we conducted a needs assessment to identify areas of need and resources?

7. What protocols and procedures does my school district have to develop formal partnerships with these organizations?

3 Crisis Response

Scenario: Student Suicide

You are the principal of a high school. On your way to work, you receive a phone call from your supervisor. They inform you that the police have reported the tragic suicide of a twelfth-grade student at your school. When they tell you the name of the student, you immediately recognize him as one of the starting varsity football players who recently suffered an injury, ending his chances of playing football competitively in college. With school starting in an hour, you realize the profound impact this news will have on both students and staff. A wave of panic begins to set in as you try to think through the necessary steps to respond to this crisis.

This scenario is every parent's and educator's worst nightmare. According to the Centers for Disease Control and Prevention (CDC), suicide is the second leading cause of death among youth, therefore the probability of a school experiencing this type of loss is high.[11] The death of a student or staff member, regardless of how it occurs, is challenging to navigate. Not only do you have to ensure that the needs of your students and staff are met quickly and effectively, but you must also manage your emotions and responses to the loss. **Crises can strike without warning, making it vital to be proactive and have a strong school-based crisis response team ready to respond when needed.**

In this chapter, we will discuss the important steps involved in responding to a school crisis. We will start with the activation of the crisis-response team, highlighting the importance of a coordinated and timely reaction. Communication is key during a crisis, so we will also explore strategies for communicating with students, families, and the broader community. This includes utilizing various communication channels effectively and managing media inquiries while maintaining confidentiality. Last, we will address providing initial support and triage for those affected by the crisis, understanding the psychological impact on students and staff, offering immediate emotional support and reassurance, and identifying signs of distress to refer individuals to appropriate resources.

Activation of the Crisis-Response Team

Now that you have identified your crisis team members, participated in training and professional development, completed a needs assessment, and established partnerships with community partners, your team is prepared to respond when a need arises. When meeting with your team to develop plans for various responses, a key component to address is the team's activation process. This plan should detail how the team will be activated during school hours, as well as before and after school hours. Additionally, the team should plan for activation during school breaks to ensure constant readiness.

Your team's activation is a vital part of your plan. When a team is activated quickly and follows established and practiced procedures, it helps initiate your response services on a more positive note. This prompt and organized activation ensures that the response efforts are effective, coordinated, and supportive right from the start, setting the tone for managing the crisis efficiently and compassionately.

Activating a school-based crisis response team can be accomplished through several methods, ensuring a quick and efficient response. In this section, we will explore various ways to achieve this. Once the team has chosen a method, they should practice the activation process to ensure everyone understands the steps and can access the notification system easily. Additionally, the team needs to discuss and include in their crisis-response plan who will be responsible for activating the team and identify a backup person to handle activation if necessary. A team can adopt a variety of activation systems. A few of those are:

Automated Alert Systems

Use automated messaging systems to send immediate alerts via text messages, emails, and phone calls to all crisis team members simultaneously. School leaders will want to check with their district to see if a platform has already been purchased that the school can utilize. If a platform does exist, or if you are going to purchase a license for your school, secure training and ensure access for your crisis team.

Mobile Apps

Implement mobile applications specifically designed for crisis management, which can send push notifications to team members' smartphones, providing instant updates and instructions.

Phone Tree

Implement a phone tree where each crisis team member has a designated partner. If one member receives an alert, they ensure their partner is also informed and ready to respond.

Email Alerts

Use a pre-set email distribution list to send out detailed instructions and information about the crisis and the assembly point. This method is not as effective as it requires members to be on their email to receive the alert.

PA System Announcements

Utilize the school's PA system to announce to staff to read their emails for important information, ensuring that everyone in the school is aware and the team can assemble quickly. **This is not a preferred method, but in certain situations, it may be needed.** You will want to practice with teachers, so they know what the announcements mean, and know to view their email without it projecting to the classroom. You will also want to remind staff of confidentiality and the importance of following processes when a crisis occurs. Sensitive and potentially frightening information (e.g., notification of a death by suicide) should *never* be announced over the PA.

Special note: If you have substitute teachers/staff in the building on the day a crisis occurs, assign someone who can go to that classroom to support the substitute and ensure they have the means to get information that may be sent out via email. This should only be done if it is safe to move throughout the building. It is recommended that the school set up a temporary username and password for substitute teachers that can be linked to the email distribution list to be used in an emergency.

Regardless of which process the team agrees upon, the principal must make sure that the team receives proper training and has access to the chosen platform. The team should practice activating the system both during and after school hours. Depending on the nature of the crisis, multiple modes of activation may be necessary and should be discussed and addressed in your crisis plan. For instance, if a crisis occurs during the school day and you need to disseminate information quickly, you may need to make an announcement instructing the team to check their email for further details or designating a location for them to assemble to discuss.

Personalized Response

In the last chapter, we discussed the need for a crisis team and the importance of having crisis plans. It is essential, however, to recognize that even though we have plans for various crises, they will always need to be adjusted and personalized based on the specifics of the event. **Every crisis is unique, and flexibility in response is key to effectively addressing the needs of students, staff, and the broader school community during such challenging times.** Below is a Crisis-Response Planning Guide that can lead the team in the development of a plan for personalized response services.

Crisis-Response Planning Guide

1. What is the nature of the crisis?
2. Has the family been notified, and do we have permission to share information with students and staff?
   - If yes, what information have they given permission to share?
   - If no, how will we support students when they are notified of the event through other means (e.g., social media, text, local media)?
   - Does the school district have policies and procedures that must be followed when sharing information about crisis events?
3. Who will be most impacted by this event?
   - Was the student or staff associated with a team, club, or organization that will impact a large group of people? If so, how will the crisis team address those specific needs?
   - Has the student or staff been at the school for a long time? Who are their closest friends or colleagues who may need additional support?
   - Has the student or staff member attended or worked at other schools that need to be contacted?
   - Does the student have siblings in the school district? If so, who will contact those schools?
4. Are there unique populations that will be impacted in ways that we need to prepare for?
   - Multilingual learners
   - Special education students
   - Online or virtual school community
   - Religious or cultural groups
5. Can the school-based crisis response team provide this support, or do we need additional help from district or state crisis teams?
   - If additional support is needed, how do we activate those supports?
   - Is there a chain of command or communication that must be followed before additional support is requested?
6. What immediate safety measures need to be implemented?

- Are there any immediate threats that must be addressed to ensure the safety of students and staff?
- Who will be responsible for leading this component of the crisis response?

7. What support services are needed for those affected?
   - What immediate emotional and psychological support can be provided to students and staff?
   - How will we identify and support individuals showing signs of distress?
   - Are there religious or cultural components we need to be aware of and sensitive to when providing support?

8. What is the best way to deliver services to students?
   - Whole class
   - Team/Club meeting (sports or academic team/clubs, advisory/ homeroom groups)
   - Small Group
   - Individual

9. Where will crisis intervention services be delivered?
   - Classroom
   - Library
   - Theater
   - Conference room
   - Other spaces where students can be spread out to maintain privacy
   - If students need to transition to specific areas, what is the process for that? What is the process for their return?

10. What supplies will be needed?
    - Food/water
    - Tissue
    - Coloring or writing materials
    - Additional supplies needed

11. How will we document and follow up on actions taken during the crisis?
    - What systems will be used to document the actions and decisions made during the crisis?

- How will we ensure thorough follow-up and evaluation of the crisis response?

12. What is the process for making referrals for ongoing services?
    - What community partners have been identified and approved to make referrals to?
    - Do we need parent permission before a referral is made?
    - How will we follow up on referrals made to ensure student and staff needs are met?
    - Is there a process or form that we will use to make and track referrals?

13. How will we determine if additional days of support are needed?
    - If additional days of support are needed, how will that be scaled?
    - If additional days of support are needed, revisit previous questions to determine ongoing need.

By addressing these questions, the crisis team can effectively personalize and adjust their plans to meet the specific needs of any given crisis. This comprehensive approach ensures that all members of the school community receive the support and care they need during challenging times, fostering a resilient and responsive school environment. By being proactive, thorough, and adaptive, the crisis team can help the school navigate through the immediate aftermath of a crisis and support the long-term recovery and well-being of students, staff, and families.

Communicating with Students, Families, and the Community

Effective communication is a cornerstone of any crisis-response plan. During a crisis, it is important to provide timely and accurate information to students, parents, and the broader community. Clear and consistent communication helps to manage anxiety, dispel rumors, and provide necessary support. **The effectiveness and timeliness of communication greatly impacts the success of any crisis response.** It can either cause panic or bring a sense of security to those affected. Utilizing various communication channels effectively is necessary to reach all stakeholders. This includes emails, phone calls, text messages, social media, and the school's website. Each channel serves a different purpose and audience, ensuring that everyone receives the information in a way that is accessible to them.

Important Note: School leaders and the crisis team must know the protocols and procedures for communication regarding crises in their school districts. Each district will have different processes and procedures the team will need to know before a crisis occurs. This process should be reviewed with the team and made part of the schools' crisis planning. For example, many school districts require consent from the parent/guardian/spouse of the deceased before any information goes out to the school community. However, information regarding the crisis event may already be spreading quickly, particularly via social media; because of this, it is important to convey that the school is aware of the event and has activated the crisis intervention and support plan. If your school district does not have written policies or protocols, it is recommended that the school leader engage in conversations with their supervisor about the need for such policies. Consistency in these protocols guarantees that families know what to expect regardless of the school their child attends, and relieves building leaders from having to make critical decisions on communication during a crisis. The Council of the Great City Schools offers a Crisis Communication guide that school districts may find useful regarding communication planning.[12]

Communicating with Students

When communicating with students, it is important to use age-appropriate language and provide reassurance about their safety and the support that is available to them. Younger students may need simpler explanations and more direct reassurance, while older students can process more complex situations. Regardless of age, all students need to feel safe, supported, and know how they can get additional help if needed.

The following guidelines can help guarantee effective communication with students:

Be Clear and Direct

Use simple, straightforward language appropriate for the student's developmental level. Avoid jargon or technical terms that may confuse them. Communication should utilize concrete language and avoid abstract terms such as "passed away." For example, instead of saying someone "passed away," use more concrete language like "died" as it is clearer and more easily understood by students.

Provide Reassurance

The most important thing to communicate with students is that they are safe and cared for. Reassure students that there are caring adults in the school who are there to help and support them.

Acknowledge Feelings

Recognize that students may have a range of emotions in response to the crisis. Let them know that it is okay to feel upset, confused, or scared and that their feelings are valid.

Encourage Questions

Encourage students to ask questions and express their concerns. Answer their questions honestly but be mindful not to overwhelm them with too much information. Avoid providing excessive details that could negatively impact their mental health and psychological safety. Dispel any rumors.

Offer Support Resources

Inform students about the support services available and how they can access additional help. Also, provide information on how they can talk to someone if they are concerned about a friend or classmate.

Follow-Up

Check in regularly with impacted students after the initial communication. Offer ongoing support and address any new concerns that may arise. Checking in with students could be as simple as greeting them in the morning and asking how they are, while other students may need designated one-on-one time with a school-based mental health professional.

Communicating with Families and the Community

Effective communication with families and the community during a crisis is important for managing the situation and providing necessary support. To ensure clear, timely, and compassionate communication, it is important to follow district protocols and policies, using pre-approved messages to maintain consistency and accuracy while respecting confidentiality. Prioritize immediate notification of families and the community, and provide regular updates as new information becomes available. Messages should be clear and concise, use straightforward language, and avoid technical jargon. Utilizing multiple communication channels, such as emails, phone calls, text messages, social media, and the school website ensures that information reaches a broad audience quickly and effectively. (See the **Sample Parent Letters** in the Resources section.)

Consistency in information is key, with all communications conveying unified messages to prevent confusion. Designating a spokesperson to handle media inquiries and public statements will help maintain consistency. Informing families about available support services, providing information on how to access these services, and how to refer someone to school-based mental health providers. Managing media inquiries should follow established guidelines, with a single point of contact (i.e., Public Information Officer, PIO) to ensure accuracy and the use of prepared statements to avoid misinformation.

As discussed earlier in this chapter, before any information is shared, the school leader must ensure that district processes and protocols regarding communication are followed. These processes and protocols should be researched in advance, incorporated into school crisis plans, and understood by all members of the crisis team. This includes guidelines for speaking with the media and posting information on social media platforms, including personal accounts. By adhering to these protocols, the school can maintain consistency, accuracy, and confidentiality in its communications.

Initial Support and Triage

Providing initial support and triage for those affected by a crisis is a multifaceted process that begins with understanding the psychological impact a crisis can have on both students and staff. Crises can evoke a range of emotions, including fear, confusion, sadness, anxiety, and anger. Recognizing these emotional responses is important for your crisis team so they can address the needs of those affected appropriately. Individuals may react differently based on their individual experiences, trauma histories, resilience levels, and the nature of the crisis. Understanding psychological principles and trauma-informed practices is imperative for effectively supporting the school community.

Given the scope of this reference guide, it is impossible to provide a comprehensive overview of psychological principles and trauma-informed practices. Instead, we will focus on common themes and offer additional resources for further exploration. **It is strongly recommended that all crisis team members undergo full training to obtain detailed information.** This section will serve as a reminder of key concepts to support effective crisis response.

The CDC's guide, *Psychology of a Crisis,* outlines four ways people process information during a crisis.[13] This information is helpful when learning about how crisis teams provide immediate support to students or staff.

People impacted by trauma tend to:

Simplify messages: This helps to avoid confusion and misinterpretation.

Cling to current beliefs: People may hold on to seemingly counterintuitive beliefs during a crisis because the brain cannot make logical sense of the current situation. Using a trusted person to deliver communication can help when working with people experiencing a crisis.

Seek additional information and opinions: During a crisis, some will want to wait to see what others are doing or get confirmation from the media before making decisions.

Trust the first message they receive: This may be the most important component for the team to remember. In a crisis, a quick response is crucial for minimizing harm. When information is lacking, people start to make speculations and fill in the gaps for information they do not have.

Understanding these processing methods is important for crisis teams, as people absorb and interpret information differently during a crisis. In other words, **focus on delivering clear, factual, and verified messages that are appropriate for the audience's age.** This approach helps to minimize confusion and ensures that the information provided is easily understood and retained.

The mental health status of those we serve will vary from person to person. However, there are key strategies the crisis team can use to support others. Some helpful strategies are:

- **Speak calmly** and maintain a soothing demeanor.
- **Repeat necessary information** as many times as needed to ensure students understand and feel reassured.

- **Provide reassurance** that they are safe and supported.
- **Offer choices** to help students feel a sense of control (for example, "Would you prefer to talk in my office or the library?").
- **Always be honest.** If you do not know the answer to a question, let them know you will work to find the answer and get back to them. As a reminder, we need to be honest while also giving information in an age-appropriate manner.
- **Validate their feelings** by acknowledging their emotions and letting them know it's okay to feel that way.
- **Use active listening skills** to show you are engaged and genuinely interested in what they are saying.
- **Encourage deep breathing or other relaxation techniques** to help manage immediate stress or anxiety.

Identifying Signs of Distress and Referring

As we have discussed, crisis team members provide immediate support to students and staff after a crisis has occurred. They meet the immediate needs of the school community while also triaging to identify people who may require additional help outside of the school. To better illustrate this concept, let's think of an emergency room (ER) at a hospital. When someone goes to the ER, they are immediately assessed by a nurse to determine their needs. Nurses look for signs of distress in their patients that will require assistance from a doctor to meet their immediate health needs. They categorize the needs of their patients by the level of care required and communicate with the necessary specialists.

Crisis counseling is very similar. The crisis team meets the immediate needs of the school community by providing a safe space and addressing mental health needs while also identifying signs of distress and making appropriate referrals to specialists either within the school district or within the community. Like a nurse, **the crisis team recognizes and provides for the immediate needs but makes appropriate referrals for ongoing care when appropriate.**

Let's go back to the scenario from the beginning of this chapter. The school-based crisis response team would provide immediate individual and/or group-based crisis response by identifying close friends of the student and meeting with them individually or in small groups. The priority for support would go to the closest friends, the football team, and the coaching staff. However, there will be members of the school community who may need more than a few days of crisis intervention support. Those closest to the student may need more directive support such as crisis counseling and therapeutic interventions. The crisis team will assess the needs and refer individuals to specialized mental health professionals within the school district or the community, ensuring they receive the necessary long-term support and care. School-based crisis response teams provide short-term crisis support while triaging for those who will need long-term interventions.

Some common signs of distress include:

Emotional Signs: Sudden mood swings, persistent sadness, anxiety, irritability, or emotional numbness.

Physical or Somatic Signs: Fatigue, headaches, stomach aches, changes in appetite, or sleep disturbances.

Behavioral Signs: Withdrawal from social interactions, changes in academic or work performance, frequent absences, or unusual risk-taking behaviors.

Cognitive Signs: Difficulty concentrating, indecisiveness, confusion, obsession with thoughts of death/dying, or intrusive thoughts about the traumatic event.

Not all signs can be identified immediately following an event and it should be noted that many of the signs above are common crisis reactions in the short term. For this reason, we do not want to over-respond (a.k.a. "over-pathologize") too quickly but instead provide guidance for adaptive coping skills. However, if these reactions continue over time and begin to interfere with functioning, a referral for more directive services is warranted. Therefore, frequent check-ins by school-based mental health professionals, school staff closest to the individual, and even peers are important. **Peer referrals play an important role, as students may notice subtle signs of distress in their friends that adults might miss.** Peer referrals are best utilized when students are taught about them proactively. They empower students to look out for one another and can be a critical lifeline for those in distress who may not feel comfortable reaching out to adults directly.

When a student is identified as needing additional support, having established partnerships with community providers can expedite the referral process, as discussed previously. Once a referral is made to the parent or guardian, the school must have a system to follow up with the parent/guardian to make sure they can connect with the outside provider. Schools should help families troubleshoot any barriers that may be present. This could include assisting with transportation, navigating insurance issues, or providing information about available resources. By maintaining open communication and offering continued support, schools can help ensure that students receive the necessary care and support from external providers.

WRAP-UP

In this chapter, we explored the steps involved in responding to a school crisis, beginning with the **activation of the crisis-response team**. We also learned about how effective **communication strategies** are vital, ensuring that timely and accurate information reaches students, families, and the broader community. This involves using various communication channels and adhering to district protocols to maintain consistency, accuracy, and confidentiality. Additionally, we covered providing **initial support and triage during a crisis**, understanding the psychological impact on those affected, and the importance of identifying signs of distress for appropriate referrals.

The crisis team's role extends beyond immediate response, offering ongoing support and making necessary referrals to specialized mental health professionals. **Recognizing signs of distress**, such as emotional, physical, behavioral, and cognitive indicators, requires frequent check-ins by school-based mental health professionals, staff, and peer referrals. We explored the value of established partnerships with community providers to expedite the referral process, ensuring that students receive ongoing care when appropriate. Maintaining open communication and offering continuous support help facilitate long-term recovery and well-being for the entire school community.

QUESTIONS to CONSIDER

1. What are the school district's policies and procedures for communicating about crisis events?

2. Who will be most impacted by the event? Was the student or staff member associated with a team, club, or organization that will impact a large group of people?

3. What is the best way to deliver services to students (e.g., whole-class, team/club meetings, small groups, individual sessions)?

4. Are there additional questions we need to include in the Crisis-Response Planning Guide specific to our school community?

5. Where can services be delivered in the case of a crisis (e.g., classroom, library, theater, conference room)?

6. How will we document support services and follow up on students needing additional support?

7. Is there additional training our crisis team needs to meet the school community's mental health needs?

4 Recovery and Continuous Improvement

Scenario: Death of a Staff Member

Early Saturday morning, you receive the heartbreaking news that Mrs. Thompson, a beloved teacher, passed away unexpectedly over the weekend due to a sudden medical condition. Mrs. Thompson has been a cornerstone at your school for over fifteen years, known for her dedication to her students and her role as the adviser for the school's debate team. Her absence will be deeply felt by students, staff, and the entire school community.

The immediate aftermath of a school crisis demands quick action from school leadership, but the journey toward recovery and continuous improvement extends well beyond the initial response. As the initial emotional shock starts to settle in, schools must begin a comprehensive path to healing, reflection, and growth. This chapter explores the significant phases of recovery and continuous improvement, exploring how schools can not only rebuild but also strengthen their resilience against future crises.

Recovery involves a series of deliberate actions aimed at restoring a sense of normalcy and emotional stability within the school. Recovery is a journey, and it builds upon the initial response. This includes providing ongoing support, facilitating open communication, and creating opportunities for reflection and connection among those impacted.

Continuous improvement, on the other hand, focuses on evaluating the effectiveness of the crisis response and identifying areas for improvement. This process requires a commitment to learning from each incident, gathering feedback from all stakeholders, and integrating those insights into updated policies and procedures. By fostering a culture of resilience and adaptability, schools can better prepare for future crises and ensure a more effective and resilient response.

This chapter delves into the multifaceted aspects of recovery and continuous improvement, offering practical guidance and real-world examples to help school leaders navigate these critical phases. From the immediate aftermath to long-term healing and policy refinement, we will explore strategies to support the emotional well-being of students and staff.

Long-Term Effects of a Crisis on the School Community

Not all school crises will have long-term impacts on the school community. Some situations will require an initial response and support, and the school community will be able to transition back into their normal routine. According to the U.S. Department of Education, the majority of students will be OK with tier 1 support systems.[14] However, there will be situations that leave a lasting imprint on the emotional, psychological, and social fabric of the school. Understanding long-term effects can help leaders develop effective and comprehensive support systems. In this section, we will explore various types of long-term effects that school crises can have on the community, including emotional, psychological, academic, behavioral, social, physical health, community, and socioeconomic effects.

School leaders and crisis teams need to be mindful of important dates that may follow an event that has impacted the school community. **Anniversary dates of the crisis, birthdays, or other important dates associated with a crisis event have the potential to have a large impact on the school community.** These dates can serve as powerful emotional triggers for students, staff, and families, often bringing back memories and feelings associated with the initial event.

To effectively support the school community during these times, leaders should proactively acknowledge these dates and plan appropriate interventions. This might include providing additional counseling services or creating spaces for individuals to express their emotions safely. It's important to recognize that everyone may respond differently; while some may seek to participate in commemorative activities, others may prefer to process their feelings privately.

By being attentive to significant dates, school leaders can demonstrate empathy and understanding, reinforcing a sense of community and support. This proactive approach can help mitigate the emotional impact and promote healing within the school community, ensuring that the school community feels supported and connected during potentially challenging times.

Leaders should be cautious in assuming what is needed in terms of support. Engaging with students and families to understand their needs and preferences for observing these dates goes a long way in building trusting and caring relationships. This collaborative approach can foster a more inclusive and responsive environment, allowing the community to navigate these emotional milestones together. The National Association of School Psychologists has developed a guide titled *Anniversaries of Traumatic Events: Guidance for Educators* that school crisis teams can add to their school crisis plans.[15]

Emotional and Psychological Effects

Crises can leave deep emotional and psychological scars on students and staff. Trauma can manifest as anxiety, depression, grief, and post-traumatic stress disorder (PTSD). Students might face difficulties concentrating, experience mood swings, or show signs of withdrawal. Similarly, staff members might struggle with burnout or secondary trauma, impacting their ability to teach and support students effectively. Remember, schools will most likely refer those individuals who need ongoing support for long-term emotional or psychological effects. A few to be aware of are:

- **Anxiety and Depression:** Students and staff may develop persistent feelings of anxiety or depression, struggling with fear, sadness, or a sense of hopelessness.
- **Post-Traumatic Stress Disorder (PTSD):** Severe crises can lead to PTSD, with symptoms such as flashbacks, nightmares, and severe anxiety that hinder daily functioning.
- **Grief and Loss:** The loss of a loved one or a traumatic event can lead to prolonged grief, affecting emotional stability and overall well-being.
- **Burnout and Secondary Trauma:** Staff members, particularly those directly involved in the crisis response, may experience burnout or secondary trauma, impacting their ability to support students.

Grief

Before we go into specific strategies to support the school family in the recovery process, I would like to take some time to discuss grief. We will explore two theories of grief that can be helpful when we work with individuals who have experienced a loss. Remember, people can grieve a variety of things that do not necessarily relate to the death of a person. People can grieve the loss of a friendship, the loss of their health, or the health of someone they love. They can even grieve their perception of safety or the end of a marriage. Understanding how a person processes grief can be exceptionally beneficial to the crisis team and even those we are supporting.

The first theory we will examine is the **Kübler-Ross Grief Cycle**. This theory, developed by Elisabeth Kübler-Ross (1969) and presented in her book *On Death and Dying*, outlines five stages of grief that people often go through after experiencing a significant loss.[16] We will explore each of these stages using our scenario at the beginning of this chapter of the death of Mrs. Thompson.

Kübler-Ross Grief Cycle

Denial

In this initial stage, individuals believe the news on Mrs. Thompson is somehow mistaken, and cling to a false, preferable reality. They may hold onto beliefs that it was not Mrs. Thompson; she was always so healthy so they must have the wrong name for the person that died. They may avoid information that contradicts this belief and seek second or third opinions.

Anger

When the individual recognizes that denial cannot continue, they become frustrated, especially at individuals closest to them. Certain psychological responses of a person undergoing this phase might be: "Why Mrs. Thompson? It's not fair!"; "How can this have happened to her, and not to me?"; "Who is to blame?"; "Why would this happen?"

Bargaining

The third stage involves the hope that the individual can avoid a cause of grief. Usually, the individual negotiates for an extended life in exchange for a reformed lifestyle. People facing less serious trauma can bargain or seek compromise.

Depression

"I'm so sad, why bother with anything? Mrs. Thompson did everything right and was such a wonderful person and she still died"; "Mrs. Thompson was the only one who understood and supported me; why go on?" During the fourth stage, the individual despairs at the recognition of their mortality. In this state, the individual may become silent, want to be alone, and spend much of their time mournful and sullen.

Acceptance

"It's going to be okay."; "I can't bring Mrs. Thompson back so I might as well accept it and do my best for her because that is what she would want me to do." In this last stage, individuals embrace mortality or the inevitable future. People who are dying may precede the survivors in this state, which typically comes with a calm, retrospective view and a stable emotional condition.

Understanding these stages helps in providing the right support at the right time. Not everyone experiences all of these stages, nor do they necessarily occur in this order. The model is not a linear timeline but a tool for understanding the experiences of those grieving.[17]

The second theory we will explore is **Worden's Four Task Model**. William Worden proposed that instead of stages, grief work can be understood as tasks that individuals need to complete to reconcile their grief and move forward.

Worden's Four Task Model

To Accept the Reality of the Loss
This task involves coming to terms with the fact that the loss is real. It often includes the initial shock and denial, and the recognition of the finality of the loss.

To Process the Pain of Grief
This task requires individuals to allow themselves to feel the pain of their loss, rather than avoid it or suppress it. It involves experiencing the full range of emotions associated with grief.

To Adjust to a World Without the Deceased
This task involves making both internal and external adjustments. Internally, it might mean redefining one's sense of self and identity in the absence of the deceased person. Externally, it includes finding new ways to function in daily life and taking on roles that the deceased person previously held.

To Find an Enduring Connection with the Deceased While Embarking on a New Life
This final task involves finding a way to stay connected with the deceased while also moving forward with life. It might include cherishing memories and continuing bonds while also engaging in new relationships and activities.

Worden's tasks provide a useful framework for understanding and supporting the grieving process. The approach emphasizes the importance of active engagement and adaptation, urging individuals to work through their grief instead of simply enduring it.[18]

By understanding and applying these theories, we can better support those in our school communities as they navigate the complex and often challenging journey of grief. This knowledge allows us to offer empathetic and informed care while fostering healing and resilience. It encourages us to create an environment where people feel safe to express their emotions, understand the grieving process, and recognize the various aspects of the grieving process. Ultimately, we aim to help them integrate their experiences into their lives in a way that honors their loss, while empowering them to move forward with hope and strength.

Crisis Support and Intervention

It is important to note that we cannot force individuals into processing their grief until they have been able to manage their crisis reactions. Being ready to process the grief can take time, and grief work often comes after crisis supports are provided to help manage and process the immediate coping challenges. Thus, in crisis response, responders can use multiple modalities of intervention based on the situation and the student population they are working with. In this section, we will review some of the more common types of intervention. In a full training model, you will learn more in-depth interventions and strategies that are appropriate for the school setting during times of crisis.

Classroom Interventions

Classroom interventions aim to provide collective healing opportunities while normalizing emotional responses and introducing strategies for the coping and grieving process. These interventions are often referred to as psychological education or psychoeducation. They focus on educating and teaching proactive mental health strategies to guide students on how to cope and seek help for themselves or their peers. In the classroom setting, crisis team members can:

- **Use Bibliotherapy for Younger Students:** Reading books that address themes of reactions, grief, and healing can help students understand and process their emotions in a relatable way. (See resource section for recommendations.)
- **Integrate Social-Emotional Learning (SEL):** Incorporating SEL into lessons allows students to develop emotional awareness and resilience.
- **Provide Announcements and Updates:** Keeping students informed about the event helps reduce anxiety and misinformation.
- **Encourage Writing Letters or Cards:** Allowing students to express their feelings by writing to the family of the deceased fosters empathy and emotional processing.
- **Facilitate Open Discussions:** Giving students space to ask questions and share with peers helps normalize emotional responses and supports collective healing.
- **Collaboration with Classroom Teacher:** Keep open lines of communication with the classroom teacher and provide them with resources that will help them respond to students based on the specific crisis event. (See the resource section for examples.)

Small-Group Interventions

Small-group interventions offer personalized support to those most affected by the crisis, creating a safe space for participants to share their emotions, stories, and memories of the deceased. These groups can include close friends, teammates, or students who have experienced previous losses that might intensify the impact of the current crisis, making it more challenging to process their feelings. These interventions focus on:

- **Group Discussions:** Facilitated conversations help students articulate their feelings and thoughts in a supportive environment.
- **Animal-Assisted Support:** Interaction with therapy animals can provide comfort and reduce stress for grieving students.
- **Sharing Memories and Stories:** Encouraging students to remember and share positive experiences with the deceased fosters connection and healing.

- **Further SEL Integration:** Continuously applying SEL principles helps students navigate their emotions.
- **Guiding Through Initial Reactions:** Allowing students to express their initial emotional responses to the event and providing strategies for managing grief.

It is important to note that discussing reactions and emotions and sharing ideas for helping each other cope is very different from processing the event (i.e. sharing your personal crisis story and experiences) which could lead to vicarious traumatization. Those facilitating group crisis interventions must be properly trained and clearly understand the difference between psychoeducational approaches and psychological processing (a.k.a. "trauma debriefing" which can cause harm when conducted inappropriately).

Individual Interventions

Individual interventions offer intensive, personalized support tailored to the unique needs of students who have been deeply impacted by the crisis event. These interventions are crucial for those requiring more focused assistance and may involve:

- **One-on-One Sessions:** Personalized plans of support are developed to address the specific needs and concerns of each student.
- **Collaboration with Families:** Working closely with families to ensure continuity of care and to make referrals for long-term support if needed.
- **Appropriate Referrals:** Providing referrals to external mental health services when additional or specialized care is necessary.
- **Follow-Up:** Crisis team members should follow up with the family to make sure they are able to connect with external mental health services. This step may require troubleshooting to remove any barriers the family may be experiencing.

Classroom, Small-Group, and Individual Intervention Strategies

Counseling Type	Focus	Strategies
Classroom	Collective healing opportunities, normalizing emotional response, strategies for the grieving process, proactive mental health strategies, and instructions on how to get help for self or peer.	• Bibliotherapy for younger students • SEL integration into classroom lessons • Announcements and updates about the event • Writing letters or cards for the family of the deceased • Allowing students to ask questions and share with their peers
Small-Group	Personalized small-group or team support, collective healing opportunities for those most impacted, creating a safe space to share emotions/impact, stories/memories of the person that has died, proactive mental health strategies, and instructions on how to get help for self or peer.	• Group discussion • Animal-assisted support • Group sharing of memories and stories of their loved one • SEL integration • Allowing students to talk through initial emotions or reactions to the event, and providing strategies to help them with the grieving process
Individual	Individualized support, intensive assistance tailored to individual needs, working with families (when needed) to make appropriate referrals for long-term care and support.	• One-on-one session with personalized plans of support • Communication with family on follow-up care • Making appropriate referrals when needed

Memorials

Memorials can serve as a way for students, staff, and the broader community to express grief and commemorate a loss or tragic event in a school setting. While memorials can play a significant role in the healing process after the death of a student or staff member, they can also be retraumatizing or lead to unintended consequences if not carefully planned. Schools should proactively develop comprehensive plans and policies for creating memorials before an emergency occurs.

The most important thing regarding memorials is the concept of "doing no harm." Memorial sites must be safe and should not retraumatize or glorify the event, particularly in cases of suicide. Schools are encouraged to consider the potential impact on the community and make decisions that foster a supportive environment. There is often debate about the appropriateness of permanent school memorials for commemorating the death of a student or staff member and their potential relevance ten to twenty years after the event. Deciding to establish a permanent memorial requires careful consideration of its impact on current students, school staff, the victim(s) family, and future students and staff.

Let's revisit our scenario for this chapter. Following Mrs. Thompson's passing, the principal decided to plant a garden in her memory. Fast forward twenty years, and those who knew Mrs. Thompson are no longer at the school. The new PTA president wants to "beautify" the school, which includes removing the neglected memorial garden. As the principal, you agree, as it has become an eyesore. However, the following summer, you receive a call from Mrs. Thompson's family, who are irate and deeply hurt that their mother's memorial has been removed.

Establishing permanent memorials sets a precedent: what is done for one must be done for all. School leaders should carefully consider and plan for such requests in advance. As educators, we want our schools to be inviting and positive spaces for learning and personal development. If school leaders are not careful, schools can start to look more like a shrine than an educational institution.

School leaders should inquire about district protocols for memorials when working on crisis planning. If district protocols are not in place, advocating for their establishment can ensure that each memorial request is handled equitably and relieves school leaders from making decisions under pressure. It also allows school leaders to focus on supporting students and staff during a crisis rather than navigating complex decisions about memorials.

Types of Memorials

Memorials can be permanent, semi-permanent, or temporary:

- **Permanent Memorials:** These include monuments, plaques, or artwork, requiring careful planning to avoid re-traumatization and address cultural or political implications. Some schools avoid permanent memorials and instead promote renewable or living memorials.

- **Semi-permanent or Living Memorials:** These might include planting trees, creating memory gardens, or establishing scholarships. They require ongoing maintenance and clear planning on how long they will remain in place.

- **Temporary Memorials:** These are often recommended for school-related deaths and can include things like memory books, temporary websites, or one-time events like candlelight vigils. Temporary memorials allow expression of grief without the long-term implications of permanent installations.

Special Considerations for Memorials After a Suicide

Memorials following a suicide require special attention and planning to prevent potential copycat behavior. It is recommended that no permanent memorials be established and that any commemoration should focus on positive action, like donations to suicide-prevention programs, volunteer activities, or raising funds for local charities. Schools should avoid large assemblies or gestures that might inadvertently glamorize the death. Schools should be mindful of suicide contagion, a phenomenon where exposure to suicide can lead to increased suicidal thoughts or actions in others.[19] The Suicide Prevention Resource Center book *After A Suicide: A Toolkit for Schools* provides helpful guidelines regarding memorials.[20]

Conducting an After-Action Evaluation of the Crisis Response

Conducting an after-action evaluation of a crisis event serves multiple significant purposes for school-based crisis-response teams. First, and most importantly, **it provides an opportunity for team members to process their emotional responses to the event**, which is crucial for maintaining their well-being and effectiveness in future interventions. Crisis work is hard! This is especially true for those who are personally impacted by the event. By reflecting on the event's impact and their roles in the response, team members can better understand their feelings and reactions, reducing the risk of burnout and secondary traumatic stress.

Second, an after-action evaluation **facilitates open communication and collaboration among team members**. It allows for the sharing of different perspectives and insights, which can lead to a more comprehensive understanding of the event and its aftermath. Since team members serve in different capacities, team reflection allows everyone to have a full picture of the event and how various parts of the crisis response impacted others. For example, if you have team members who deliver classroom support, they may have valuable feedback for those who send students to and from the class for individual support.

This approach helps identify strengths and areas for improvement in the crisis response, enabling the team to refine their strategies and enhance their preparedness for future crises. Debriefing serves as a learning opportunity for the entire school community. By analyzing what worked well and what could be improved, the team can develop best practices and guidelines that inform future crisis-response efforts. This continuous learning process helps build a more resilient school environment, ensuring that the community is better equipped to handle future challenges.

Finally, an after-action reflection process can **reinforce a sense of community and support among staff and students and help attend to longer-term needs and considerations**. It demonstrates the school's commitment to caring for the well-being of everyone involved, fostering trust and confidence in the crisis-response process. By addressing concerns and validating emotions, this process helps create a supportive atmosphere where individuals feel heard and understood.

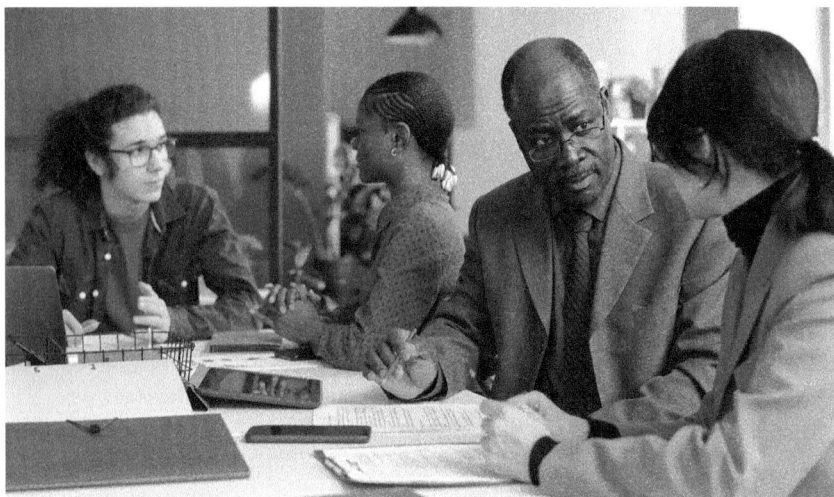

Steps to Guide After-Action Reflection and Evaluation

As a part of your crisis plan, school and crisis team members should develop a systemic process for after-action reflection in advance. When this becomes a regular part of the crisis-response process, it becomes second nature to constantly evaluate the services and encourage connection and support for all team members. Below are some suggestions for debriefing.

Gather the Team

While assembling all members of the crisis-response team as soon as possible after the event to make daily next-step decisions is important, it is often more helpful to engage in in-depth reflection after some time has passed when the crisis team members have had time to recover and reflect on their experiences. It is important to ensure that everyone involved in the response has the opportunity to participate in the after-action reflection.

Create a Safe Environment

Set a tone of openness and confidentiality, emphasizing that the after-action reflection is a safe space for expressing thoughts and emotions without judgment. This is essential for encouraging honest and constructive dialogue. This may take time to develop as relationships are built with each event.

Review the Event

Start by summarizing the facts of the event to ensure everyone has a shared understanding of what occurred. This includes the timeline, actions taken, and outcomes observed.

Discuss Emotional Responses

Allow team members to share their emotional reactions to the event. Encourage everyone to express how the crisis impacted them personally and professionally, helping to normalize these feelings.

Evaluate the Response

Analyze the effectiveness of the response efforts. Discuss what strategies worked well and what challenges were encountered. This evaluation should be objective and focused on improving future responses. Leaders should be prepared for how they will address situations that may become challenging. Emotional responses are normal, but the leader must be prepared to ensure the environment is emotionally safe.

Identify Lessons Learned

Highlight key takeaways from the event and the response. Identify any gaps in the current crisis plan and discuss potential adjustments or enhancements.

Develop an Action Plan

Based on the lessons learned, outline specific steps to improve the crisis-response plan. Assign responsibilities for implementing these changes and set a timeline for follow-up.

Provide Support Resources

Offer information about support services available to team members who may need additional help processing the event. This could include counseling services or stress management workshops.

Conclude with Positivity

End the reflection with words of appreciation for the team's efforts and commitment. Reinforce the value of their work and the importance of supporting each other. Taking time to uplift and support crisis responders will go a long way in building relationships, creating a culture of trust and respect, as well as building long-standing capacity within your team.

By following these suggestions, crisis-response teams can make sure these sessions are effective and supportive, and lead to actionable improvements in their response strategies. This approach helps create a culture of continuous learning and adaptation, which is essential for navigating the complexities of crisis management. In the end, these initiatives help establish a safer and more resilient school environment, better prepared to assist students and staff during future difficulties.

WRAP-UP

In the aftermath of a school crisis, the immediate response from leadership sets the tone for healing, but the path to recovery and continuous improvement extends far beyond initial actions. As the emotional shock begins to settle, schools must embark on a comprehensive journey of healing, reflection, and growth. **Recovery** involves deliberate actions to restore normalcy and emotional stability within the school community, including ongoing support, open communication, and opportunities for reflection. Meanwhile, **continuous improvement** focuses on evaluating the crisis response, identifying areas for enhancement, and integrating feedback from stakeholders into updated policies. By fostering a culture of resilience and adaptability, schools can strengthen their preparedness for future crises.

Understanding the **long-term effects of a crisis** is essential for developing effective support systems. While some crises allow for a return to normalcy, others leave lasting emotional, psychological, and social imprints. School leaders and crisis teams must be mindful of significant dates, such as anniversaries or birthdays, which can trigger emotional responses. Proactively acknowledging these dates and planning appropriate interventions, such as additional supports or spaces for emotional expression, can promote healing. Engaging with students and families to understand their needs and preferences helps create a collaborative and responsive environment, supporting the community through these emotional milestones.

Emotional and psychological effects of crises, such as anxiety, depression, grief, and post-traumatic stress disorder (PTSD), can deeply impact students and staff. Schools should be prepared to refer individuals needing ongoing support to external mental health services. The chapter explores two theories of grief: **Kübler-Ross's Grief Cycle**, which outlines five stages of grief, and **Worden's Four Task Model**, which emphasizes tasks for reconciling grief.

The chapter also examines various intervention modalities, including **classroom, small group, and individual interventions**, each tailored to the situation and student population. Classroom interventions focus on collective healing and proactive mental health strategies, while small-group interventions offer personalized support and safe spaces for sharing emotions. Individual interventions provide intensive support tailored to unique needs, involving one-on-one sessions and collaboration with families. Additionally, the chapter addresses **memorial management**, emphasizing the importance of planning memorials that do no harm and are sensitive to the community's needs. Finally, the chapter highlights conducting a **debriefing after a crisis** as essential for processing emotional responses, facilitating communication, and identifying improvement areas, ensuring schools are better equipped for future challenges.

QUESTIONS to CONSIDER

1. What systems are currently in place to provide ongoing emotional support to students and staff following a crisis?

2. How can we ensure that all members of the school community feel heard and supported during the recovery process?

3. What are our strategies for identifying and supporting individuals who may experience long-term emotional or psychological effects from a crisis?

4. How do we evaluate the effectiveness of our crisis-response efforts? What metrics or feedback mechanisms are used to assess our performance?

5. How do we incorporate lessons learned from past crises into our future crisis plans and protocols?

6. Are there district policies or protocols on memorials? If not, who can I collaborate with to establish those?

7. What is our process for conducting debriefings after a crisis event, and how do we ensure that all team members have the opportunity to participate?

8. How do we foster a culture of open communication and continuous learning within our crisis-response team?

5 Caring for Educators and Self (Listen, Care, Connect)

Scenario: School Shooting

Several classes are out on the playground at Maple Grove Elementary School for recess when an irate parent, Mr. Williams, who recently had his parental rights removed, storms onto the playground with a gun, demanding to see his children. The teachers quickly try to gather the students and lead them back into the building. As they do, Mr. Williams begins firing his gun, hitting a third grader, Emma, in the leg, and tragically killing a beloved teacher, Ms. Hernandez, who had stepped in front of the students to protect them. Amid the chaos, the remaining teachers manage to get the rest of the students inside, initiating a lockdown as law enforcement arrives on the scene. The student body, staff, and families are heavily impacted.

We've covered a lot about crisis work so far, including the makeup and preparation of a school-based crisis response team, understanding trauma and grief responses, supporting students based on their level of impact, and triaging them for effective mental health support. Now, let's shift our focus to caring for the educators in your school who have been affected by the crisis and need additional support as well.

Just as importantly, we need to explore ways to care for ourselves during this challenging time. You read that correctly! We will spend time in this chapter focused on **how to care for the caregivers and that certainly includes you**. A wise person once told me that if I did not care for myself in crisis work, no one would, and then who would be there to help the students? Recognizing when to pause and address your own needs is one of the most challenging aspects of crisis work. In this chapter, we will explore how to recognize the signs that the caregivers in your school are struggling and detail strategies for meeting those needs.

Recognizing and Addressing the Impact of Crisis Response on Educators and Self

When a crisis occurs within a school, the immediate focus is often on the students, as it should be. However, it's equally important to acknowledge and address the impact that such events have on front-line educators. Teachers, counselors, administrators, and support staff all play pivotal roles during a crisis, often setting their own emotional and psychological needs aside to support their students. Over time, this selfless dedication can take a significant toll on their well-being, impacting their personal and professional lives.

Educators are not immune to the effects of trauma. In fact, they often experience what is known as "vicarious trauma" or "secondary traumatic stress," which occurs when they are exposed to the trauma of others, particularly their students. This exposure can lead to symptoms like those experienced by the students they are trying to help, including anxiety, depression, and burnout. **The pressure to maintain a calm and composed demeanor while managing their own emotional responses can be overwhelming.** Recognizing these signs in oneself and one's colleagues is the first step in addressing the impact of crisis response on educators.

Self-awareness is key to recognizing the impact of crisis work on your own mental and emotional health. Educators are often conditioned to prioritize the needs of their students above their own, which can lead to neglecting their own well-being. However, just as the safety instructions on an airplane advise putting on your oxygen mask before helping others, educators must ensure that they care for themselves to effectively support their students.

Self-care is not a luxury in crisis work; it is a necessity. It involves taking deliberate actions to maintain your physical, emotional, and mental health. This can include basic practices like getting enough sleep, eating well, and exercising regularly. It also involves setting boundaries, taking time to decompress, and seeking support from colleagues, friends, or mental health professionals when needed. Regularly reflecting on your emotional state and stress levels can help you identify when you need to take a step back and prioritize your own well-being.

Identifying Signs in Yourself

One of the most important steps in maintaining your well-being during and after a crisis is recognizing when you need extra support. This can be challenging, especially for educators who are often focused on caring for others. However, paying attention to the following signs in yourself can help you identify when it's time to seek help:

Physical Symptoms

Stress and emotional strain often manifest physically. Frequent headaches, stomach issues, unexplained aches and pains, or a persistent feeling of fatigue can all be indicators that your body is responding to emotional distress.

Changes in Sleep Patterns

Difficulty falling asleep, waking up frequently during the night, or sleeping too much can be signs of stress or anxiety. Conversely, needing excessive sleep or feeling like you can't get enough rest may also indicate that your body is struggling to cope with emotional strain.

Emotional Instability

Feeling more irritable, anxious, or sad than usual, or experiencing mood swings, can be red flags that you are struggling to manage your emotions. If you find yourself crying easily, feeling overwhelmed, snapping at those you love, or experiencing a sense of hopelessness, these may be signs that you need to stop and take care of yourself.

Difficulty Concentrating

If you're having trouble focusing on tasks, making decisions, or remembering things, it could be a sign that your mind is preoccupied with stress or trauma. This cognitive strain can impact your ability to perform your job effectively and may indicate that you need to take a step back.

Withdrawal from Others

If you notice yourself pulling away from colleagues, friends, or family, it may be a sign that you're feeling overwhelmed. Isolation can exacerbate feelings of stress and anxiety, making it harder to cope.

Loss of Interest or Motivation

If you find that you're no longer interested in activities you once enjoyed, or if you're struggling to find motivation to complete everyday tasks, it may be a sign that your emotional health is suffering.

Substance Use

Turning to alcohol or other substances to cope with stress is a clear sign that you may need extra support. While it might seem like a temporary escape, substance use can lead to more significant issues and should be addressed as soon as possible.

If you recognize any of these signs in yourself or a colleague, it's important to take action. For yourself, this might mean reaching out to a trusted friend, colleague, or mental health professional to discuss your feelings and explore ways to manage your stress. Don't hesitate to take advantage of resources like an Employee Assistance Program (EAP), counseling services, or even taking some time off to recharge. Leading by example is powerful, and those you lead will be watching to see if you take steps to care for yourself during this time.

Recognizing Signs in a Colleague

Just as it's important to recognize signs of distress in yourself, it's equally crucial to be aware of similar signs in your colleagues and administrators (who are often overlooked due to the strong focus placed on supporting teachers and staff). Supporting each other during and after a crisis can create a stronger, more resilient school community. However, before responding to a colleague who may be struggling, think about who the best person may be to address them and when is the best time. We want our colleagues to know they are cared for and valued. Here are some signs that a colleague may need extra support:

Changes in Behavior

If a normally energetic and engaged colleague becomes withdrawn, irritable, or unusually quiet, it could be a sign that they are struggling. Conversely, someone who is typically reserved but becomes unusually outspoken or emotional may also be showing signs of distress.

Decline in Job Performance

A noticeable drop in a colleague's job performance—such as missing deadlines, making frequent mistakes, or seeming disorganized—can be an indicator that they are overwhelmed or distracted by personal stressors.

Frequent Absences or Tardiness

A colleague who begins to frequently call in sick, arrive late, or leave early may be struggling with the emotional impact of a crisis. These absences can be a sign that they are finding it difficult to manage their workload and personal well-being.

Increased Irritability or Conflict

If a colleague who is usually calm and collected begins to react with frustration or anger, or if they start having conflicts with other staff members, it may be a sign that they are under significant stress.

Withdrawal from Social Interactions

A colleague who isolates themselves, avoids staff meetings, or declines invitations to socialize may be trying to cope with feelings of being overwhelmed or emotionally drained.

Expressing Hopelessness or Despair

If a colleague makes comments that suggest they are feeling hopeless, overly pessimistic, or that they believe their efforts are meaningless, it's a strong signal that they need support. These comments should be taken seriously and addressed with care.

When it comes to a colleague, approach the situation with empathy and concern. You might start a conversation by expressing what you've noticed and offering your support. For example, you could say, "I've noticed that you seem a bit more stressed lately. Is there anything I can do to help, or would you like to talk about it?" Sometimes, simply knowing that someone cares can make a significant difference. Encourage them to seek support if they need it and remind them that it's okay to ask for help.

Strategies for Managing Stress and Preventing Burnout

Managing stress and preventing burnout are deeply personal processes, as everyone experiences stress differently and has unique ways of coping. What works well for one person might not be as effective for another. Therefore, it's important to understand that stress management is not a one-size-fits-all approach. The key is to find strategies that resonate with you, fit into your lifestyle, and genuinely help you maintain your well-being.

While the specifics may vary, some general strategies are effective for many people. These approaches can serve as a starting point for developing your own personalized stress management plan.

Establish a Routine

Having a consistent daily routine can provide a sense of stability and control, which is especially important during times of stress. Start your day with a morning routine that sets a positive tone, whether that's through exercise, meditation, or simply enjoying a quiet cup of coffee. Ending your day with a calming evening routine can help signal to your body that it's time to unwind.

Practice Mindfulness and Meditation

Mindfulness practices, such as meditation, deep breathing exercises, or yoga, can be highly effective in reducing stress. These practices encourage you to focus on the present moment, which can help you manage anxiety and prevent your mind from becoming overwhelmed by worries about the past or future. Even a few minutes of mindfulness each day can make a significant difference in how you handle stress.

Physical Activity

Regular physical activity is one of the most effective ways to combat stress. Exercise releases endorphins, the body's natural stress relievers, and can improve your mood, energy levels, and overall health. Whether it's a walk, a workout at the gym, or a dance class, find an activity that you enjoy and start moving.

Set Boundaries

Setting clear boundaries between work and personal life is the foundation for preventing burnout. This might involve limiting the hours you spend on work-related tasks, saying no to additional responsibilities when you're already stretched too thin, or creating a designated workspace that you can leave at the end of the day. Boundaries help protect your time and energy, ensuring that you have space for rest. Realizing that you cannot be everything for everyone can be liberating, and it is the best thing you can do for your mental and physical health.

Stay Connected

Social support is a powerful buffer against stress. Make time to connect with friends, family, and colleagues who uplift and support you. Whether through in-person visits, phone calls, or video chats, maintaining these connections can provide emotional support, offer different perspectives, and remind you that you're not alone in your experiences.

Practice Self-Compassion

It's easy to be hard on yourself, especially when you're feeling stressed or overwhelmed. Practicing self-compassion involves treating yourself with the same kindness and understanding that you would offer to a friend. Acknowledge that it's okay to feel stressed, that you're doing your best, and that taking care of yourself is not selfish but necessary.

Prioritize Rest and Sleep

Sleep is fundamental to stress management and overall health. Make sleep a priority by establishing a regular bedtime routine, creating a restful environment, and avoiding stimulants like caffeine close to bedtime. Quality rest allows your body and mind to recover from the day's stresses.

Engage in Creative Activities

Creative outlets, such as drawing, journaling, playing music, or crafting, can be incredibly therapeutic. These activities allow you to express your emotions, process your thoughts, and focus your mind on something enjoyable and fulfilling. Even if you don't consider yourself "creative," finding a hobby that brings you joy can significantly reduce stress.

Seek Professional Support

If stress becomes overwhelming or persistent, it may be helpful to seek support from a mental health professional. Therapists and counselors can provide guidance, teach coping strategies, and offer a safe space to express your feelings. Professional support is particularly important if you notice signs of burnout, such as chronic exhaustion, feelings of detachment, or a loss of motivation.

Let's revisit our scenario from the beginning of this chapter. A situation like the one at Maple Grove Elementary would demand all hands on deck to support the significant needs of both the students and their families. With police and media on the scene, the staff and school leadership would find themselves pulled in many directions. The response and student support efforts would likely extend over a long period, creating sustained pressure and exposure to trauma. The impact would be immense for all employees, especially those tasked with supporting the mental health needs of others. If the mental health needs of the staff and administrators are not addressed, they will not be able to provide the prolonged support the students will need.

So how do you do that as a leader? I am so glad you asked!

Listen, Care, and Connect

Leaders need to understand that most, if not all, of the mental health professionals in your school, are not trained to provide mental health services to adults. Their formal training focuses on providing services to children and adolescents. However, in the aftermath of a crisis, the emotional and psychological needs of the adults within the school community—teachers, staff, and administrators—cannot be overlooked. This is where the *Listen, Care, and Connect* approach becomes invaluable.

LISTEN   **CARE**   **CONNECT**

LISTEN: Creating a Space for Voices to Be Heard

The first step in supporting staff after a crisis is to actively listen. This means creating opportunities for staff members to express their thoughts, feelings, and concerns without fear of judgment or repercussion. It's not just about hearing words but truly understanding the underlying emotions and experiences. Crisis team members should facilitate open forums, small-group discussions, or one-on-one meetings where staff can talk about how the crisis has impacted them.

Active listening also involves being present in these conversations—setting aside distractions and focusing entirely on the person speaking. By doing this, leaders can better gauge the emotional climate of their staff, identify those who may be struggling more than others, and begin to build trust. This trust is what builds further care and connection.

CARE: Showing Empathy and Offering Support

Once staff members have been given the space to share their experiences, the next step is to show care through empathy and tangible support. Crisis team members should acknowledge the emotions and challenges that staff are facing, validating their feelings rather than dismissing them. It's important to recognize that different individuals will react to stress and trauma in different ways, and there is no "right" or "wrong" way to feel after a crisis.

Caring also involves offering support in various forms, whether that's through providing mental health resources, adjusting workloads, or simply offering a compassionate ear. Crisis team members and leaders can demonstrate care by checking in regularly with staff members, asking how they are doing, and making it clear that their well-being is a priority. Small gestures, such as providing a quiet space for reflection or organizing wellness activities, can also go a long way in showing that the school cares about its staff.

CONNECT: Building a Network of Support

Finally, connection is about fostering a sense of community and ensuring that no one feels isolated in their struggles. Leaders should encourage staff to connect with one another, creating a supportive network where individuals can lean on their colleagues for emotional and practical support. Peer support groups can facilitate this, along with team-building activities and simply encouraging open communication among staff.

Leaders and crisis team members will also need to connect staff with external resources, such as local mental health professionals, to provide additional support that may be beyond the school's internal capabilities. As mentioned, the majority of school-based mental health professionals do not have certifications or training for providing mental health support to adults. Therefore, it is important that we listen to the staff, let them know that we care about them, and then connect them to community-based mental health resources that can provide the specialized care they need. This approach ensures that staff receive the appropriate level of support, helping them to cope with the emotional challenges they face while continuing to care for their students and themselves.

Let *Listen, Care, and Connect* be a motto by which you serve when working with adult mental health. The school cannot be everything to everyone. That is too heavy a lift, and trying to live up to that expectation will certainly lead to burnout. *Listen, Care and Connect* can help us set good boundaries for ourselves when supporting staff. You can find more information on facilitating psychological recovery on the National Child Traumatic Stress Recovery Network website.[21]

WRAP-UP

After a crisis, it's normal for educators and staff to focus on meeting students' immediate needs and getting back to a sense of normalcy. However, it's equally important to remember that those on the front lines of the crisis response also need care and support. Seeking help after a crisis isn't a sign of weakness; in fact, it's essential for maintaining your mental health and overall well-being.

Support can take many forms, whether it's talking with colleagues who understand what you've been through or seeking professional counseling from a licensed mental health provider. It's important to acknowledge that processing the emotional toll of a crisis takes time, and everyone's healing process looks different. By engaging with support networks, you can better manage stress, process your experiences, and prevent long-term effects like burnout or secondary traumatic stress.

As leaders and crisis team members focus on their staff's mental health, they must also take time to reflect on how the crisis has affected them personally. Those responsible for supporting others' mental health are especially vulnerable to secondary trauma. It's crucial to remember you matter, too. Your mental health should be a priority. While your school or district could replace you in your professional role (a tough reality to accept), no one can replace you as a spouse, parent, child, or friend. The roles you play in your personal life are unique, and the people who love and depend on you need you to be well.

Taking care of yourself isn't just an important part of providing effective crisis support; it's the most important thing you can do for yourself and those closest to you. By prioritizing your own mental health, you ensure you can continue serving others while maintaining the balance and well-being necessary for all areas of your life.

QUESTIONS to CONSIDER

1. What strategies does your school currently have in place to support the mental health of educators during and after a crisis? Are they listed in your crisis plan?

2. How can you integrate self-care practices into your daily routine to better manage stress and prevent burnout? What specific actions can you take to prioritize your well-being?

3. In what ways can you and your leadership team foster a culture of support and empathy among staff members during times of crisis?

4. How can you ensure that every staff member feels heard, cared for, and connected?

5. What external resources (e.g., local mental health professionals) are available to support your staff, and how can you better utilize these resources to provide specialized care?

6. Does your district have an Employee Assistance Program (EAP)? If so, how can you connect employees with EAP?

7. Are there boundaries that need to be set or adjusted to prevent burnout among crisis team members and staff? How can you communicate and enforce these boundaries in a way that supports the well-being of everyone involved?

6

Bringing It All Together: Navigating a Crisis Scenario

Navigating a Crisis Scenario

Now that we have explored the key components of crisis response and the formation of your crisis team, let's walk through a full crisis scenario. This will allow you to see how the concepts we've covered come together, guiding you to address and minimize the psychological impact on your school community during times of crisis.

In Chapter 3, we started with the following scenario:

> You are the principal of a high school, and on your way to work, you receive a phone call from your supervisor. They inform you that the police have reported the tragic suicide of a twelfth-grade student at your school. As they tell you the name of the student, you immediately recognize him as one of the starting varsity football players who recently suffered an injury, ending his chances of playing football competitively in college. With school starting in an hour, you realize the profound impact this news will have on both students and staff. A wave of panic begins to set in as you try to think through the necessary steps to respond to this crisis.

There's no question that this is an incredibly challenging situation to navigate as a school leader or crisis-response lead. Sadly, I've worked with many schools that have faced this exact circumstance, and it is always a profoundly difficult experience for everyone involved. Even with prior crisis training, the emotional impact of a student or staff member's suicide can leave us feeling overwhelmed, making it difficult to recall the necessary steps to support the school community. With that in mind, let's apply the knowledge from this book and work through this situation together.

As the School Principal

1. Contact your School-Bases Crisis Response Team Leader.

Contact your School-Based Crisis Response Team Leader to review the information you have gathered so far.

2. Notify other school leaders.

Notify other school leaders (e.g., administrators and school mental health professionals) and brief them on the situation.

3. Remind the Crisis Team leader to use the pre-established crisis plan as a *guide*.

We know that each crisis is unique, and your pre-established plan will more than likely need to be customized given the specifics of the crisis. Having the crisis plan serves as the foundation of your response, but flexibility allows your school-based crisis response team leader the ability to make impactful alterations where needed.

- Give them the flexibility to **adapt the plan as needed**, especially when it comes to supporting student and staff mental health. Trust their expertise. They are the lead at your school for a reason and are trained to provide mental health support in a variety of settings.
- Delegate the responsibility for student and staff support to the school-based crisis response leader so they can begin preparing for the day.

4. **Instruct your Leadership Team to meet in your office as soon as they arrive to conduct a debriefing.**

   Encourage anyone who can come in early to do so. In this scenario, you have little time before school starts and some of your leadership team may not be able to adjust so quickly to the start of school. Share the facts with as many team members as you can in person, and phone conference with the others so they are getting important first-hand information. This helps to avoid misunderstandings and misinformation.

5. **Send a message to Staff.**

   Send a message to Staff via the communication platform outlined in your crisis plan (e.g., text, messaging app, phone tree). Avoid disclosing specific details, but include the following:

   - "We will be holding a mandatory meeting before school at _____ time to discuss a loss in our school community. We know this is a difficult way to start the day, but we want to ensure you have the information and support you need."
   - You may have to hold multiple sessions to ensure all staff can meet with you. Especially for those staff who may not have the ability to come to school early.

6. **During the Leadership meeting, provide a quick overview of the situation.**

   During the Leadership meeting, provide a quick overview of the situation. Collaboratively **identify staff and students who were close to the student.** In this scenario, the student was on the football team, so **additional support** for the coaching staff and players would be essential.

- Assign a crisis team member to find a space for the football team to gather shortly after the school day begins.
- Call the head coach to brief them on the situation. Stress that communication with the family has not yet occurred, so details shared with students will be minimal. The coach may have already heard from the family or other players. It is important to get any information they may have.
- Ask the head coach to inform the other football coaches and ensure they can be with the team during the meeting.

7. **At the Staff meeting...**

At the Staff meeting, it's likely that many will have already heard the news, as information spreads quickly. Assume that some students and staff may already know more than you do.

- As principal, start the meeting by sharing as complete a **summary of the situation** as we are allowed to at this time. Since contact with the student's family hasn't been made, instruct staff to be cautious about what is shared with students. Inform them that information shared in this staff meeting is confidential and we want to minimize additional harm to the family.
- Emphasize that we are **still obtaining information** so we will not be focusing on how the student died. Instead, focus on acknowledging the loss, validating emotions, and closely monitoring those who struggle the most.
- **Reassure staff** that support will be available for them as well. Remind everyone that we are a school family, and it's okay to express emotions during this difficult time.
- Remind staff **not to post information on social media**, even personal social media accounts, about the student's death. Remind staff why it is important to maintain confidentiality in order to respect the family and all who care for the student.
- After providing incident facts, the **Crisis Team Leader then outlines the plan for emotional support** throughout the day.
- Assign one of your assistant principals, or other members of your leadership team, to **meet with any staff who were not able to come into school early** so they are informed when they sign in for the school day.

8. **Draft a statement to use if anyone calls the school.**

    After the Staff meeting, draft a statement for front office staff to use if anyone calls the school seeking information.

    – A **sample statement** could be: "Thank you for your call. We appreciate your concern for our students and staff. Out of respect for the family, we are unable to provide additional information at this time. Crisis counselors will be available today to support students and staff, and the principal will send out a letter via email with more information to families."
    (If you plan on sending out information via another platform, you can replace email with the communication platform you will be using.)

    – Make sure your front office (and other key support staff) knows the student and staff support plan for the day. You will also want to make sure they know how to get help if they need to speak with someone. Support staff play a crucial role within the school and can often have deep relationships with both students and staff. As most school leaders know, the support staff is often the glue that holds the school together and it is important to remember that they will need support as well.

9. **Prepare a statement that will be read to the students.**

    Prepare a statement, in collaboration with your Crisis Team Leader, that will be read to students in first period. Once students start to arrive you will quickly be able to tell if the student body has information about the death of their classmate.

    – When preparing a statement, do not be afraid to let who you are as a leader come through. Your statement should connect with students emotionally and ensure they are not alone during this time. If there is time, have a few crisis team members develop a list of FAQs that students are more likely to ask. This helps with consistency in providing an appropriate response and decreases the anxiety of the crisis team member and/or teacher reading the statement.

    – Having a moment of silence is appropriate.

    – Following a moment of silence, instruct students on how they can get help to talk to a counselor.

10. **Monitor common areas closely for struggling students.**

Ensure that hallways, public spaces, and other areas where students may gather are monitored throughout the day. This responsibility can be shared with assigned crisis team members.

- If you encounter students lingering in these spaces who appear to be struggling with the loss, gently **guide them to the crisis center**, where they can speak with a mental health professional.
- Making a **personal connection** is essential during times of loss. Walking with students to the crisis center, and engaging in supportive conversation along the way, can help them feel safe and more comfortable opening up to counselors or other trusted adults.
- Often, students will want to set up a **memorial** for their friend. For example, students may want to leave notes on the deceased student's locker and place items in front of or on the locker. Let students know that at the end of the day, you will collect the notes and will provide them to the family (ask your Crisis Team to screen the notes to make sure they are appropriate to share with the family). This allows students a space to grieve and honor their friend while not committing to a semi-permanent memorial. (Remember the information shared earlier in this book on memorials.)

11. **Take a moment to breathe.**

At this stage, you've engaged with leadership, staff, and students. Pause to gather your thoughts and calm yourself before reaching out to the family. Practicing self-care is crucial, as the emotional weight of this process can be overwhelming.

12. **Contact the family of the student.**

When contacting the family, speak directly with a parent or guardian (or preferred family member the family has assigned as the point of contact). Offer your sincere condolences, answer any questions, and request permission to send a letter to the school community.

- This will be an exceptionally hard conversation to have. Before you call, **make a list** of things you want to say or questions you need to ask.

- It will be important to **ask what they are comfortable sharing** and how they would like to communicate with the school to ensure the facts are accurately conveyed. Providing an overview of the next steps the school plans on taking to provide support for the school community is important to ensure that your response takes cultural sensitivities into consideration.

- Let them know that **ongoing communication** is important as decisions are made for how to honor their loved one and that the school wants to ensure they are respecting the family's wishes. (Note: this will be important as memorial service decisions are made, and also regarding what to do with the student's belongings—some parents may want the belongings delivered to the home while others may want to come to school to retrieve the belongings. Be aware that the timing for this may differ greatly with families and some families may not be ready to talk about their child's belongings right away.)

- Should **family members prefer to come to the school** themselves, coordinate a time after school hours to ensure privacy, allowing them the space to grieve without additional disruptions.

13. **Draft a letter that will be sent home with students.**

    Draft a letter in collaboration with your Crisis Lead that will be sent home with students or via electronic delivery. (See the **Sample Parent Letters** in the Resources section.)

    - If the family does not want a letter to be sent home with identifying information, you must respect their wishes. In the letter, you would state that you had a loss in the school family, but out of respect for the privacy of the family, no additional information will be shared at this time. However, student support services will be available to students.

    - Include helpful, age-appropriate information for parents on discussing grief and loss with their children, and provide contact details for school supports.

    - Mention any available community resources that offer mental health counseling support.

14. **Check in with your Crisis Team.**

    Make sure they do not need any additional support and let them know how much you appreciate them. Often, Crisis Team members will not bring anything to eat because they are trying to get to the school as soon as possible. If funds are available, or if community organizations volunteer, provide meals for your crisis team (and other staff helping with the crisis response, if funds allow).

- Crisis response can be emotionally taxing. Your support and acknowledgment as the principal can have a significant impact, empowering the team to continue supporting the community throughout the day.
- Continue to check in periodically for updates and to ensure team well-being.

15. Schedule a Crisis Team after-school meeting.

Arrange a time with the crisis team for an end-of-day reflection and planning for the next day. A staff meeting may also be valuable to collect reflections from teachers and staff and to provide additional support if needed.

- During the meeting, discuss what went well, additional needs, any required adjustments, and whether extended support days from the crisis team are warranted.
- Thank the crisis responders and the crisis lead for their work. Crisis work is exceptionally difficult and small gestures can make a big impact on their mental health.

16. Meet with your Leadership Team and plan for upcoming needs.

Gather your Leadership Team to review the day's events and discuss anticipated needs. This is also a good time to determine who from the school will attend the visitation services to show support on behalf of the school.

- Some school Leadership Teams choose to create a schedule to ensure an administrator is present at the visitation services throughout, providing a familiar and supportive presence for students who may attend without family or friends.

As the Crisis Team Leader

1. **Gather and confirm information from your school principal.**

    – Work with the principal or administration to **confirm the student's identity and circumstances** without sharing details unnecessarily. Handle all information with the utmost confidentiality.

    – **Determine the need for crisis responders** based on the information that you have received. In this scenario, given the student's grade level and school involvement, you can expect the need to be high, so you will want to activate or request from district support, if available, additional crisis responders for this event.

    – Check the student information system for your district to **determine whether the student has siblings or other close family members who attend another school**. If they do, inform the leadership team and decide who will contact the sibling's school administrator or school counselor to inform them of the death.

2. **Activate the Crisis Team.**

    – **Notify and mobilize crisis responders** based on the pre-established communication format in your crisis plan.

    – Give crisis responders a **brief overview**, and inform them where to meet, and what time to arrive. It is also good practice to remind responders to keep the information confidential.

    – **Develop an overview of the needs and assign responders to specific roles** (signing students in and out of the crisis center, providing group crisis interventions, individual crisis interventions, classroom meetings, etc.).

3. **Prepare for the Crisis Response to ensure that your team has everything they need to provide student and staff support.**

   – **Communicate** with crisis team colleagues on space for the crisis support.

   – **Gather** sign-in/sign-out sheets, pens, tissues, hall passes, etc. that will be used throughout the day. If your team needs a walkie-talkie to maintain communication with the principal or other school personnel, secure those as well.

   – **Meet with the crisis team** at the time specified and review the plan for the day. Inform each crisis team member of their role and answer any questions they may have. For this situation, assign several (if possible 5–6) crisis responders to the location where the football team will meet separately from the rest of the student body.
   Special Note: Crisis members who have been through formal crisis training should be assigned to this task. Given the situation and the number of students involved, you will need trained crisis responders to lead this support. If you have more than one school crisis lead, you will want to send one of the leaders with the crisis responders to guide the response.

   – **Give the crisis team a script of the event** and what can/cannot be shared with students.

   – Inform them of the process of **how to get students assessed for mental health distress,** if needed. Follow any district policy and procedures that may exist for this step.

   – While support for those closest to the student (like the football team) is essential, it's also helpful to **identify and monitor other students or staff** who may have had recent losses, mental health struggles, or those prone to heightened emotional responses to such events.

4. **Prepare communication with the Principal that will be shared with students and staff.**

   – **Get input/approval from the PIO**, or Public Information Officer.

   – In collaboration with administration, **draft a message for staff to be shared before school begins**, notifying them of the student's passing without providing explicit details. Emphasize the importance of confidentiality.

- **Prepare a message for students**, crafted with sensitivity, to be read in classrooms by crisis team members or by teachers. Avoid mention of suicide specifics and focus instead on acknowledging the loss and offering support options.

- **Develop a letter for parents**, with the family's permission, to inform them of the loss, the availability of counseling resources, and guidance on discussing grief with children. (See sample letter). Follow any district procedures or processes that may be established in this situation.

5. **Remain flexible so that you can adjust the level of support as needed.**

Leading the crisis response will shift based on the needs of your student body and staff. Anytime you deal with a student death, especially one that died by suicide, your plan must remain flexible so that you can adjust your level of support as needed.

- After the principal talks with the staff, **give staff information on how to respond to students**, and provide helpful tips on how to address the news with students, respond to emotional reactions, and maintain a supportive atmosphere. (See the *Talking Points When Addressing Families and How to Support Their Grieving Child* in the Resources section.)

  - Emphasize the **availability of crisis support for both students and staff** and encourage staff members to monitor students for signs of distress. Review common reactions to be expected as well as those reactions that necessitate an immediate referral to the school mental health/crisis team.

  - Review with the staff how they can **refer students to the crisis/counseling center** and any procedures they need to be aware of for the day.

  - Communicate to students and staff in a way that **reduces the risk of suicide contagion** (i.e., when exposure to suicide may increase the risk in others). Avoid explicit details, focus on grief support, and discourage any glorification of the incident.

- **Assign a responder to follow the student's schedule for the day** and be in the classroom to help the teachers.

- Determine **individual and/or groups of students for whom proactively reaching out with interventions** and supports may mitigate emotional impact.
- For those who self-refer or are referred by staff, **have a crisis/counseling center staffed with mental health crisis team members**. If possible, maintain space between conversations to offer some privacy.
- **Check on responders** throughout the day and monitor any additional needs that may arise. Help responders troubleshoot any situation that may present itself throughout the day.
- Periodically **check in with the principal** and give updates on the response.

6. **Document the crisis response throughout the day.**

   Keep details of what students were seen, follow-up needs of students, any communication that was made to families, etc. **Keep detailed records** of all actions taken, team member roles, and communications sent. This documentation is essential for assessing the crisis response and planning for future needs.

7. **Lead an end-of-day meeting with Crisis Team members and the Administration Team.**
   - Gather the Crisis Team at the end of the day to review the day's support efforts, **identify any remaining needs, and adjust plans** if necessary.
   - Discuss any **follow-up support** that might be needed for specific students or groups in the coming days or weeks, including additional crisis support or mental health referrals.
   - Discuss what went well, what needs adjustments, and ways to improve for future events.
   - Make sure to **thank your team** for their work. Crisis work is difficult and whenever possible, lift your team up.

WRAP-UP

Every crisis is unique, bringing its own challenges and requiring flexibility in your response. This chapter breaks down what a real-life crisis response might look like, focusing on how to **navigate each step when an unexpected tragedy hits a school**. By using the scenario at the beginning of the chapter, you can role-play with your team to practice what you'd do in a similar situation. Practicing together builds confidence and prepares your team to work smoothly and support each other when every moment counts.

Throughout this book, each chapter opens with a new crisis scenario to help guide these practice sessions. This approach allows your team to walk through the varied aspects of crisis response—from initial notification and communication to providing emotional support and managing logistics. **Role-playing** helps each team member understand their role, develop quick problem-solving skills, and gain the experience to make better, faster decisions under pressure. Teams can add components to the scenario to make it fit the school environment that you work in (for example, if you have multilingual learners, if you do not have assistant principals, or are in an alternative environment).

By investing time in these **practice scenarios**, you will build a stronger, more resilient team that can rely on each other during difficult times. When everyone knows the plan and feels comfortable with their role, it's easier to stay calm and focused, which has a powerful, calming effect on the entire school community. Practicing together not only sharpens your team's skills but also strengthens trust and communication, which are essential when emotions are high and quick action is needed. In the end, a well-prepared team is better equipped to provide steady, compassionate support, helping the school community heal and move forward.

In crisis situations, **preparation and flexibility go hand-in-hand**, and this chapter—and the book as a whole—aims to help you build both, empowering you to respond with confidence and compassion when your school community needs it most. By embracing the strategies and practices outlined here, you're not only strengthening your team's crisis response, but also fostering a culture of resilience, empathy, and support that will serve your students, staff, and families well in any challenge that comes your way.

QUESTIONS to CONSIDER

1. What elements of the scenario in this chapter would be most challenging for your team, and how might you address them in practice sessions?

2. How could you modify the scenario presented in this chapter to reflect unique aspects of your school (e.g., language needs, community demographics, resources)? How might these modifications affect your team's approach to a similar crisis?

3. What are some ways to prevent misinformation while still keeping everyone in the loop?

4. Staff are often the first to notice when students are struggling. What training or resources could you offer teachers and support staff to help them identify signs of distress, especially after a traumatic event? How can you encourage staff to reach out for help themselves when they are affected?

5. In this chapter, the principal and crisis lead focus on creating spaces for staff and students to process grief and access support. In your school environment, what additional steps could be taken to support students who may need individual attention or are hesitant to reach out for help?

6. How often can you commit to going through scenarios with your leadership and crisis team? Can you schedule those sessions now so it is a priority on everyone's calendar?

Conclusion

I vividly remember being called to work for my first school-based crisis response. I was terrified! The last thing I wanted was to accidentally make things worse for students because I didn't know the right words to say. But with each crisis call, my confidence grew. I realized that, more than anything, students need someone to be present with them in those difficult moments—someone to show compassion, to reassure them that what they're feeling is normal, and to let them know it's okay to grieve.

For many students, this may be the first time they've lost someone they knew and loved or experienced a tragedy that impacted them personally. As part of the school support team, it's up to us to be there for them in whatever ways they need. Sometimes that means offering a quiet space for them to sit with their feelings, and other times it means listening to their questions or letting them know it's okay to feel confused or angry. **I've learned that just showing up, being present, and letting them know they're not alone can make a world of difference.**

I also realized early on that you don't always need the perfect words— sometimes, just being there is enough. Students notice when adults are genuine, and even when we don't have all the answers, they feel it when we care. The most important thing is to meet them where they are, to reassure them that their feelings are valid, and to let them know that it's okay to take things one day at a time.

When I was in high school, one of my classmates died on her way to school in a terrible car crash. I did not know her well, but it had a significant impact on me. I can still hear the principal's voice breaking as he announced it over the intercom. All around me, classmates were crying, some sobbing uncontrollably, and even the teachers were devastated. I remember feeling overwhelmed with sadness and not understanding why—I hadn't been close to her, but the sense of loss was everywhere. We have come a long way since then, as we have learned that surprising students and staff with devastating news via an intercom can increase traumatic impact. But we have also learned how to be proactive and reach out to those most impacted instead of waiting for them to reach out to adults for help.

Looking back now, I see how our school pulled together to help us through it. Healing didn't just happen by chance. My school had planned for a crisis like this long before it ever happened, and our crisis responders had training that prepared them for that difficult day. But, most importantly, we had adults who cared deeply and showed up for us. They didn't leave us to figure it out alone; they were right there with us, guiding us through the hard days that followed her death. **That experience taught me just how powerful a prepared and compassionate support system can be in helping a community heal.**

In school-based crisis work, you don't need to know everything about mental health, trauma, or grief. What's important is surrounding yourself with people who do, and people who have been trained in school-based crisis response. It's all about having a solid team you can count on when things get tough. Each person brings something different to the table, so, together, you can cover all the bases and make sure students and staff get the support they need.

It takes a special person to lead crisis work. It takes someone who understands the complexity of emotions, the gravity of the situation, and the unique needs of each individual. You have to be prepared, yet flexible, able to think on your feet, and maintain calm amid the chaos. In crisis work, every situation is different, requiring a leader who can adapt strategies in real-time, showing empathy, resilience, and dedication to helping others find a path forward. That person is YOU!

So, as you are stepping into this work, remember: **it's not about having all the answers—it's about being the calm in the storm and offering a steady presence when everything else feels uncertain.** You have the power to help others find their way through the darkness. That strength, that heart for others, that willingness to be there no matter what—that's what makes you the person students and staff can lean on during hard times.

Take a deep breath. Develop your plan in collaboration with a strong team. Make training a priority for you and your team.

You can do this work!

Michelle

Resources

Where can I find more information about school-based crisis response and training?

PREPaRE Crisis Training Curriculum

https://www.nasponline.org/professional-development/prepare-training-curriculum

The **PREPaRE Crisis Training Curriculum**, developed by the National Association of School Psychologists (NASP), is a comprehensive, evidence-based program designed specifically to equip school professionals to effectively respond to a variety of school crisis situations. PREPaRE is featured in the Best Practices Registry of the Suicide Prevention Resource Center. The name *PREPaRE* stands for:

- **P**revent and prepare for psychological trauma
- **R**eaffirm physical health, security, and safety
- **E**valuate psychological trauma risk
- **P**rovide interventions and respond to psychological needs
- **a**nd
- **R**espond to psychological needs
- **E**xamine the effectiveness of crisis prevention and intervention

The curriculum comprises two primary workshops:

Workshop 1: *Crisis Prevention and Preparedness: Comprehensive School Safety Planning*

In this one-day workshop, participants will learn how to establish and sustain comprehensive school safety efforts that attend to both physical and psychological safety. The workshop addresses critical components needed to develop, exercise, and evaluate safety and crisis teams and emergency operations plans (EOPs), including building vulnerability assessments. The model also integrates school personnel and community provider roles in providing school-based crisis preparedness and response activities. Additional topics addressed include media/social media, communication, reunification, students with special needs, culture, and memorials. After this workshop, participants will be better prepared to improve their school's climate, student resilience, and crisis-response capabilities of school personnel. This workshop makes a clear connection between ongoing crisis prevention, mitigation, protection, response, and recovery. This workshop benefits a broad range of school staff and administrators who are engaged in safety and crisis-response work.

Workshop 2: *Crisis Intervention and Recovery: The Roles of School-Based Mental Health Professionals*

In this two-day workshop, participants will develop the knowledge and skills required to provide immediate mental health crisis interventions to the students, staff, and school community members who have been simultaneously exposed to an acute traumatic stressor. Various individual and group crisis-intervention supports are taught based on a multi-tiered approach. The knowledge and skills developed within this session also help to build a bridge to the psychotherapeutic and trauma-informed mental health response required to address challenges associated with trauma exposure. This training is intended for school and community mental health professionals and crisis team members who will be providing psychological support after a crisis.

There is also corresponding **Training of Trainers (ToT) workshops** to develop local capacity for ongoing sustainability and training.

International Critical Incident Stress Foundation (ICISF)

https://icisf.org

The **International Critical Incident Stress Foundation (ICISF)** offers comprehensive training programs centered around Critical Incident Stress Management (CISM). These courses are designed to equip participants with practical skills for crisis intervention and disaster behavioral health, serving emergency responders, healthcare professionals, and other community members.

Key training options include:

- **Core CISM Courses**: Foundational courses such as *Assisting Individuals in Crisis* and *Group Crisis Intervention* provide techniques for addressing different crisis scenarios effectively.
- **Specialized Programs**: The ICISF also offers targeted courses like *CISM Application with Children*, *Managing School Crises*, and workshops focused on resilience and peer counseling.
- **Certificate of Specialized Training**: Participants can earn certificates documenting their expertise in specific areas of CISM after completing required coursework.
- **Training Modalities**: Courses are available in various formats, including in-person, virtual, and asynchronous online options. Virtual training often features live interactions with instructors and practical exercises for skill development.

These courses are part of ICISF's mission to enhance crisis-response capabilities, promote wellness, and foster community resilience in facing critical incidents.

National Center for School Crisis and Bereavement (NCSCB)

https://www.schoolcrisiscenter.org

The **National Center for School Crisis and Bereavement (NCSCB)** supports schools in managing crises and student grief. Their training includes guidance on pre-crisis preparation, immediate response, and long-term recovery, emphasizing the emotional and psychological needs of students and staff. They provide resources for crisis management plans, grief support, and recovery strategies tailored to educational environments. NCSCB also collaborates with schools to offer practical tools and consultation services during and after crises to facilitate effective support and recovery efforts.

Safe and Sound Schools

https://safeandsoundschools.org

Safe and Sound Schools provides comprehensive training programs focused on school safety and crisis preparedness. Their offerings emphasize a holistic approach, integrating emergency planning, response strategies, and recovery processes. Training covers best practices for enhancing school safety infrastructure, fostering community collaboration, and preparing for a variety of emergency scenarios. Programs are designed to empower school administrators, teachers, and safety officers with the knowledge and skills needed to ensure student and staff safety and well-being.

Especially Safe Program

https://safeandsoundschools.org/programs/especially-safe

The **Especially Safe Program** from Safe and Sound Schools focuses on protecting vulnerable and special-needs student populations during emergencies. It provides tailored safety resources, training, and strategies for educators and school staff to enhance the safety and preparedness for students with unique needs. The program emphasizes collaboration, practical planning, and inclusive practices to ensure comprehensive safety measures for all students.

"I Love U Guys" Foundation

https://iloveuguys.org

The **"I Love U Guys" Foundation** provides essential training programs to enhance school and community safety. Their **Standard Response Protocol (SRP)** offers a consistent, actionable plan using five core actions—Hold, Secure, Lockdown, Evacuate, and Shelter—to respond effectively to various incidents.

Additionally, their **Standard Reunification Method (SRM)** guides the safe and structured reunification of students with guardians after a crisis. The foundation offers training sessions, from half-day to full-day workshops, equipping educators, administrators, and first responders with the skills to implement SRP and SRM in their schools. Widely adopted and research-backed, these programs aim to create safer school environments.

Where can I find additional information about how crises impact students?

American School Counselor Association (ASCA)

https://www.schoolcounselor.org

They provide resources and articles focused on crisis response and supporting students through trauma. Visit their website for relevant materials and guidelines.

National Child Traumatic Stress Network (NCTSN)

https://www.nctsn.org

NCTSN offers detailed resources on trauma, including the effects of crises on students and strategies for support. Explore their website for reports and tools tailored to schools.

Substance Abuse and Mental Health Services Administration (SAMHSA)

https://www.samhsa.gov

Their resources include guides on handling trauma and building resilience among youth. Access their materials on their website.

Child Mind Institute

https://childmind.org

This organization provides insights into how different types of trauma affect children and what educators and caregivers can do to support them. Visit their website for practical advice and research findings.

National Association of School Psychologists (NASP)

https://www.nasponline.org/resources-and-publications/resources-and-podcasts/school-safety-and-crisis

They have crisis response and intervention resources specifically designed for school settings. Check out their guidance at the link above.

Readiness and Emergency Management for Schools (REMS)

https://rems.ed.gov

The US Department of Education's Office of Safe and Supportive Schools REMS TA Center provides resources to build preparedness capacity (including prevention, protection, mitigation, response, and recovery efforts) of schools, school districts, institutions of higher ed (IHE), and their community partners at the local, state, and Federal levels. Resources include crisis planning and response resources and tabletop scenarios for practice can be found on their website.

I want to use a MTSS model for student support during times of crisis. Where can I find resources to help my team implement tiered levels of support for students?

These resources are ideal for schools looking to strengthen their crisis-response capabilities through an MTSS framework, being mindful to create a proactive, multi-level approach to supporting students' well-being and resilience.

National Center on Safe Supportive Learning Environments (NCSSLE)

https://safesupportivelearning.ed.gov

- Resources: Offers a variety of resources and tools for integrating MTSS into school safety and crisis-response plans. Their materials provide guidance on applying MTSS frameworks to support students' social-emotional and mental health needs during and after crises.

Center on Positive Behavioral Interventions and Supports (PBIS)

https://www.pbis.org

- **Overview**: PBIS is a key component of MTSS, and the center provides resources for implementing tiered support systems that incorporate crisis response and trauma-informed practices.
- **Specific Tools:**
  - Resources on developing school-wide support systems that include tiered interventions for emotional and behavioral crisis response.
  - Guides and case studies on using PBIS frameworks for effective crisis management.

The Collaborative for Academic, Social, and Emotional Learning (CASEL)

https://casel.org

- **Focus**: CASEL's resources help integrate social-emotional learning (SEL) into the MTSS framework, supporting students' mental health and resilience during crises.
- **Application**: Guidance on using MTSS for school-wide SEL implementation and targeted support to help students cope with crisis situations.

National Association of School Psychologists (NASP)

https://www.nasponline.org

- **MTSS and Crisis Response Resources**: NASP provides publications and guidelines on how MTSS can be used in crisis response to provide tiered support. Their materials include recommendations for universal support (Tier 1), targeted interventions (Tier 2), and intensive interventions (Tier 3).
- **Key Features**: Emphasizes the importance of a cross-disciplinary team approach for effective crisis intervention and recovery within an MTSS framework.

The Center for MH in Schools & Student/Learning Supports (UCLA)

https://smhp.psych.ucla.edu

- **Comprehensive Approach**: This center offers resources on how MTSS can incorporate mental health supports, particularly during crisis situations. Their guides address the need for integrated support systems that leverage school and community resources.

- **Materials**: Practical advice for aligning MTSS with school-based crisis response teams and community crisis response.

American School Counselor Association (ASCA)

https://www.schoolcounselor.org

- **MTSS and Crisis Intervention Guidance**: ASCA provides specific resources and training materials on implementing MTSS in schools, including its use in crisis intervention. It covers how school counselors can play a critical role in each tier of the MTSS framework during a crisis.
- **Professional Development**: Webinars and workshops on integrating MTSS into school counseling programs to support crisis response.

Safe and Civil Schools

https://www.safeandcivilschools.com

- **Training and Resources**: Offers professional development and resources focusing on creating safe, positive, and proactive school environments through MTSS frameworks. These programs include training on preparing for and responding to crises.
- **Workshops**: Tailored workshops that incorporate positive behavioral support and crisis-response strategies within an MTSS model.

Sample Parent Letter #1

(Not Including Details Per Family Request)

<DATE>

Dear Parent/Guardian,

It is with heavy hearts and with deep sadness that we inform you about a loss to the <Insert School Name> School family. Out of respect for the privacy of the family through this extremely difficult time, we cannot share additional information about the student per the family's request. However, we know that some students may learn of this loss through various social groups and want to provide families with support and resources.

This loss might raise many emotions, concerns, and questions for our entire school, especially with our students. Our goal is to assist our school family in understanding grief and to provide some helpful suggestions for coping. Our school mental health professionals and our district crisis team will be available to offer support and resources to groups and individuals as needed. Please feel free to reach out to discuss any concerns/questions with one of the school staff members listed below.

Principal: <Insert Name and Email.>

Counselors: <Insert Name and Email. If applicable, list which counselor serves specific populations.>

<Any Other Mental Health Staff>

The National Help Line is also available 24/7 for crisis support and serves individuals of all ages. The number for the helpline is 1-800-273-8255. We also recognize that you, as parents, may want to help your child as they cope with this loss. At the bottom of this letter, you will find some suggestions for talking with your child about grief, as well as a list of community resources. Thank you for your support and for being a part of our <Insert School Name> School family.

Sincerely,

<Insert Name>, Principal

Note: A list of ways to talk to children about grief by developmental level can be found at:

- The Dougy Center for parents and staff
  https://www.dougy.org/assets/uploads/Developmental-Responses-to-Grief-ages-2-18.pdf
- SAMHSA tips for families and staff after a tragic event
  https://www.samhsa.gov/sites/default/files/tips-talking-to-children-after-traumatic-event.pdf
- National Association of School Psychology has talking tip sheets for a variety of audiences with resources in Spanish and English
  https://bit.ly/3NVFwH9

15-Minute Focus: School-Based Crisis Response:Understanding, Preparing For, and Recovering From Crisis Events by Michelle Sircy
© National Center for Youth Issues www.ncyi.org

108

15-MINUTE FOCUS
School-Based Crisis Response:
Understanding, Preparing For, and Recovering From Crisis Events

Sample Parent Letter #2

(With Additional Details)*

<DATE>

Dear Parent/Guardian,

It is with heavy hearts and deep sadness that we inform you about a loss to our <Insert School Name>
School family. Last night, <insert name with permission>_ was killed in a car accident. We wish to express
our heartfelt sympathy to the <Insert Family's Last Name>_ family and thank them for allowing us to share in
their life. This loss might raise many emotions, concerns, and questions for our entire school, especially our
students.

Our goal is to assist our school family in understanding grief and to provide some helpful suggestions for
coping. <Insert School Name> staff are available to offer support and resources. If you need support, please
contact a designated staff member listed below. District crisis responders will also be available to offer
individual counseling support to our students.

Principal: <Insert Name and Email.>

Counselors: <Insert Name and Email. If applicable, list which counselor serves specific populations.>

<Any Other Mental Health Staff>

We also recognize that you, as parents, may want to help your child as they cope with this loss. Attached to
this letter you will find some suggestions for talking with your child about grief, as well as a list of community
resources. As always, our staff will be available to address any concerns you have now or in the future.

Sincerely,

<Insert Name>, Principal

* Only include information for which the family gives permission.

15-Minute Focus: School-Based Crisis Response:Understanding, Preparing For, and Recovering From Crisis Events by Michelle Sircy
© National Center for Youth Issues www.ncyi.org

* Only include information for which the family gives permission.

Media Talking Points When Addressing Families and How to Support Their Grieving Child

This is a sample talking guide if the school leader is asked to talk to the media about ways families can support their grieving child.

This is not easy! Talking about death and grief is one of the most difficult things we will do as parents. A few tips to help our families through this process are:

- It is important for parents to remember that **all children react to grief differently**. Some kids may cry, become angry or anxious, or they may not have any reaction at all and that is OK. Grief is an individual journey and everyone does not grieve the same way.

- As parents we often want to say the perfect thing to help our children and to take the hurt away. But the best thing we can do is to **listen and comfort our children** through loss. Remember, your child does not need you to be perfect, they just need you to be present with them and to help them through this difficult time.

- When talking to your child about death, **use simple, clear words** and avoid using language that is not concrete. For example, younger children may not know what you mean if you say someone has "passed away." Use words that are simple and direct.

- **Allow your child to talk about death and ask questions**. Answer questions as simply as you can. And remember that it's ok to say that you don't know how to answer all of the questions.

- **Resume your regular family/school activities and schedules** as soon as possible. Routines are one good way to help your child feel secure.

- If this is your **child's first experience with funeral/memorial services**, explain the process to them and what they can expect while at the funeral.

- Most importantly, **monitor your child's stress level**. During times of grief, stress is expected. However, prolonged stress or sadness may be indicators that your child is struggling and needs some additional support. If you have any questions, do not hesitate to reach out to your child's school counselor or physician.

Crisis Team: We develop an individual plan for each crisis event depending on the details of the incident and the grade level of the students impacted. Our main goal is to help students process difficult information, give them positive coping skills, and triage students who may need more intensive counseling interventions.

Bibliotherapy for Young Students

The Invisible String by Patrice Karst
A comforting story about connection, even when loved ones are far away or have passed on.

Lifetimes: The Beautiful Way to Explain Death to Children by Bryan Mellonie and Robert Ingpen
A gentle book that explains the concept of life cycles in nature.

I Miss You: A First Look at Death by Pat Thomas
This book addresses feelings children may have after a loss, aiming to normalize their experiences.

The Goodbye Book by Todd Parr
Simple language and colorful illustrations help children understand saying goodbye and experiencing loss.

When Dinosaurs Die: A Guide to Understanding Death by Laurie Krasny Brown and Marc Brown
Explains death in a straightforward way for younger children, covering different types of loss and emotions.

A Terrible Thing Happened by Margaret M. Holmes
For children who have witnessed trauma, this book follows Sherman the raccoon as he processes his feelings and learns to cope.

Something Bad Happened: A Kid's Guide to Coping with Events in the News by Dawn Huebner
A gentle book explaining how children can process scary events they may hear about.

The Day My Daddy Lost His Temper by Dr. Carol Ann Loehr
A book that helps children understand and deal with adult emotions that can be frightening for them.

The Tenth Good Thing About Barney by Judith Viorst
A story about a young boy coping with the death of his cat and remembering the positive memories.

Goodbye Mousie by Robie H. Harris
For young children experiencing the death of a pet, helping them understand grief and say goodbye.

Ida, Always by Caron Levis and Charles Santoso
Inspired by two real-life zoo polar bears, this story is about friendship, loss, and the power of memory.

The Memory Box: A Book About Grief by Joanna Rowland
A child collects memories of a loved one, reinforcing the idea that memories keep those we've lost close to us.

What Happens When A Loved One Dies? by Dr. Jillian Roberts
Simple and clear explanations on death and what might happen afterward, offering reassurance.

DOWNLOADABLE RESOURCES

The resources in this book are available to you as a digital download!

Please visit **15minutefocusseries.com** and click this book cover on the page. Once you've clicked the book cover, a prompt will ask you for a code to unlock the activities.

Please enter code:

CRISIS574

Endnotes

1   "PREPaRE Training Curriculum," National Association of School Psychologists (NASP), n.d., https://www.nasponline.org/professional-development/prepare-training-curriculum.

2   National Prevention Framework, "National Prevention Framework," National Prevention Framework, Second Edition, June 2016, https://www.fema.gov/sites/default/files/2020-04/National_Prevention_Framework2nd-june2016.pdf.

3   "When Is It Permissible to Utilize FERPA's Health or Safety Emergency Exception for Disclosures? | Protecting Student Privacy," n.d., https://studentprivacy.ed.gov/faq/when-it-permissible-utilize-ferpas-health-or-safety-emergency-exception-disclosures.

4   FindLaw. 2002. "Find Laws, Legal Information, and Attorneys - FindLaw." Findlaw. 2002. https://www.findlaw.com/.

5   "Justia," Justia, October 13, 2024, https://www.justia.com/.

6   "Home," n.d., https://www.nsba.org/.

7   Education Law Association, "Landing • Education Law Association," May 7, 2024, https://www.educationlaw.org/.

8   Safe and Sound Schools, "Programs - Safe and Sound Schools," July 13, 2023, https://safeandsoundschools.org/programs/.

9   "Home ♥ the 'I Love U Guys' Foundation," n.d., https://iloveuguys.org/.

10   National Center for School Mental Health, School Mental Health Quality Guide: Needs Assessment & Resource Mapping, National Center for School Mental Health, 2023, https://www.schoolmentalhealth.org/media/som/microsites/ncsmh/documents/quality-guides/Needs-Assessment-&-Resource-Mapping.pdf.

11   "WISQARS Leading Causes of Death Visualization Tool," Centers for Disease Control and Prevention, n.d., https://wisqars.cdc.gov/lcd/?o=LCD&y1=2022&y2=2022&ct=10&cc=ALL&g=00&s=0&r=0&ry=2&e=0&ar=lcd1age&at=groups&ag=lcd1age&a1=0&a2=199.

12   "Crisis Communication: Before, During, and after a Crisis or Active Shooter Event a Guidebook for Public Relations Executives in the Council of the Great City Schools." 2023. https://www.cgcs.org/cms/lib/DC00001581/Centricity/domain/35/publication%20docs/CrisisCommGuidebook2023.pdf.

13   CERC, Psychology of a Crisis, Psychology of a Crisis, 2019, https://emergency.cdc.gov/cerc/ppt/CERC_Psychology_of_a_Crisis.pdf.

14   Miguel Cardona, "Supporting Child and Student Social, Emotional, Behavioral, and Mental Health Needs." U.S. Department of Education, 2021. https://www.ed.gov/sites/ed/files/documents/students/supporting-child-student-social-emotional-behavioral-mental-health.pdf. p. 25.

15   "Anniversaries of Traumatic Events: Guidance for Educators," National Association of School Psychologists (NASP), n.d., https://www.nasponline.org/resources-and-publications/resources-and-podcasts/school-safety-and-crisis/mental-health-resources/anniversaries-of-traumatic-events-guidance-for-educators.

16   Elisabeth Kübler-Ross, On Death and Dying (New York: The Macmillan Company, 1969).

17   Ross, Death and Dying.

18   William J. Worden, Grief Counseling and Grief Therapy : A Handbook for the Mental Health Practitioner. Fifth edition. (New York, NY: Springer Publishing Company, 2018).

19   "Risk and Protective Factors for Suicide," Suicide Prevention, April 25, 2024, https://www.cdc.gov/suicide/risk-factors/?CDC_AAref_Val=https://www.cdc.gov/suicide/factors/index.html.

20   Doreen S. Marshall et al., After a Suicide: A Toolkit for Schools, Second Edition, n.d., https://sprc.org/wp-content/uploads/2022/12/AfteraSuicideToolkitforSchools-3.pdf.

21   Sarah Peterson, "About SPR," The National Child Traumatic Stress Network, March 18, 2020, https://www.nctsn.org/treatments-and-practices/psychological-first-aid-and-skills-for-psychological-recovery/about-spr.

About the Author

DR. MICHELLE SIRCY is the Program Coordinator for Comprehensive School Counseling at the Kentucky Department of Education, bringing more than 23 years of dedicated experience in public education. Her distinguished career has been marked by a steadfast commitment to advancing mental health services, strengthening crisis response protocols, and promoting equity in schools. Dr. Sircy's professional journey has encompassed roles as a middle school special education teacher, high school counselor, and school counseling specialist for one of the nation's largest school districts, where she led a team of over 300 school counselors for more than a decade.

A recognized authority in crisis response, Dr. Sircy led a large district crisis team for over ten years, coordinating support for more than 450 crisis events to ensure that students, staff, and families received timely and necessary care and support. She has also consulted on numerous crisis response needs statewide, expanding her influence throughout Kentucky. Her leadership has also extended statewide as the crisis support lead for the Kentucky Counseling Association. Additionally, she spearheaded suicide prevention initiatives in her school district, impacting over 400,000 students and adults.

Beyond her work in K-12 settings, Dr. Sircy is an adjunct professor at Spalding University, where she teaches school-based crisis response and small-group counseling. An active contributor to her field, she has written for the American School Counseling Association and co-authored the Kentucky Framework of Best Practices for School Counselors. A passionate advocate for equity, she frequently presents at the American School Counseling Association (ASCA) on essential topics like equity, data-driven counseling, and comprehensive school counseling programs.

Dr. Sircy's impact continues to shape school-based crisis response and mental health advocacy, fostering resilient, inclusive, and supportive learning environments for students and educators alike.

A Brief Look At Michelle's Sessions

School-Based Crisis Response

Unfortunately, the likelihood of school leaders encountering a crisis event during their tenure is high. Being well-prepared for crisis response equips school staff with the ability to think quickly and critically when such situations arise. In this session, participants will gain a comprehensive understanding of how to effectively respond to crises within a school setting. School counselors, administrators, and educators will explore best practices and strategies to ensure the safety and mental well-being of students and staff during times of crisis.

This session is not a replacement for crisis prevention but provides attendees with skills and a knowledge base on how to respond once a crisis has occurred. The session will include interactive activities, case studies, and practical tools that participants can immediately apply to their school environments.

Attendees will learn how to:

- Develop a crisis response plan tailored to their school's unique population.
- Clearly define roles and responsibilities for school crisis team members to ensure coordinated and efficient responses.
- Communicate effectively with students, staff, and parents during and after a crisis.
- Foster a supportive and resilient school climate that can withstand and recover from crises.

Data-Driven School Counseling and Student Supports

In this session learn how to leverage data to enhance school counseling and student support services. In today's educational landscape, data-driven approaches are essential for identifying student needs, measuring the effectiveness of interventions, and ensuring equitable outcomes for all students.

Through hands-on activities, real-world examples, and practical tools, attendees will gain the skills necessary to integrate data into their daily practice. This session is designed to empower school counselors to make informed decisions, optimize their support services, and ultimately enhance student success. Whether you're new to data-driven approaches or looking to refine your existing practices, this session will provide valuable insights and actionable strategies.

Attendees will learn how to:

- Understand the importance of data in school counseling and how it should drive decision-making processes.
- Collect and analyze relevant data to identify student needs and monitor progress.
- Use data to develop targeted interventions that address academic, social-emotional, and college/career challenges.
- Implement data-driven strategies to support diverse student populations and promote equity within the school community.

Equity-Driven School Counseling

This interactive session focuses on empowering school counselors to become proactive allies in addressing inequities within their school communities. Through a blend of discussion, reflection, and practical strategies, participants will learn how to:

- Identify ways school counselors can be active allies through data driven approaches to address inequities.
- Discuss proactive racial equity strategies to support students and lead change within your school and community.
- Strategize ways to lead classroom lessons, small groups and individual sessions to increase students' understanding of their identity and those different from them.
- Identify the ASCA Ethical Standards for School Counselors and the ASCA Student Standards: Mindsets & Behaviors for Student Success related to the school counselor's role in racial equity.

15-minute focus

Brief Counseling
Techniques that Work

Look for these books in the series!

REGULATION AND CO-REGULATION
Accessible Neuroscience and Connection
Strategies that Bring Calm into the Classroom

Ginger Healy

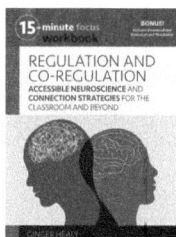

REGULATION AND CO-REGULATION WORKBOOK
Accessible Neuroscience and Connection
Strategies for the Classroom and Beyond

Ginger Healy

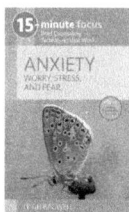

ANXIETY
Worry, Stress, and Fear

Dr. Leigh Bagwell

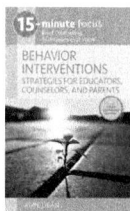

ANXIETY WORKBOOK
Tips and Strategies to manage Anxiety, Build
Resilience, and Foster Emotional Well-Being

Dr. Leigh Bagwell

BEHAVIOR INTERVENTIONS
Strategies for Educators,
Counselors, and Parents

Amie Dean

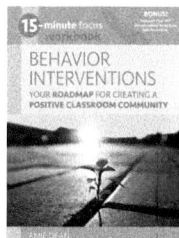

BEHAVIOR INTERVENTIONS WORKBOOK
Your Roadmap for Creating a
Positive Classroom Community

Amie Dean

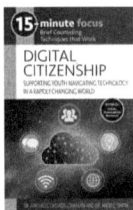

DIGITAL CITIZENSHIP
Supporting Youth Navigating
Technology in a Rapidly
Changing World

Dr. Raychelle Cassada Lohmann
and Dr. Angie Smith

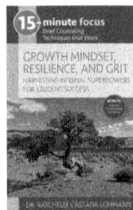

GROWTH MINDSET,
RESILIENCE, AND GRIT
Harnessing Internal Superpowers
for Student Success

Dr. Raychelle Cassada Lohmann

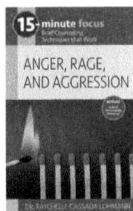

ANGER, RAGE, AND AGGRESSION

Dr. Raychelle Cassada Lohmann

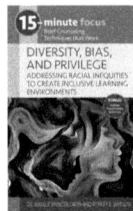

DIVERSITY, BIAS, AND PRIVILEGE
Addressing Racial Inequities
to Create Inclusive Learning
Environments

Dr. Natalie Spencer Gwyn
and Robert B. Jamison

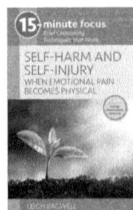

SELF-HARM AND SELF-INJURY
When Emotional Pain
Becomes Physical

Dr. Leigh Bagwell

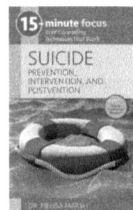

SUICIDE
Prevention, Intervention,
and Postvention

Dr. Melisa Marsh

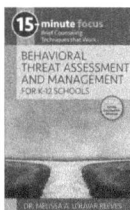

**BEHAVIORAL THREAT
ASSESSMENT AND MANAGEMENT
for K-12 Schools**

Dr. Melissa A. Louvar Reeves

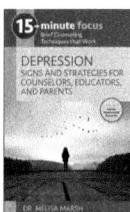

**TRAUMA
and Adverse Childhood
Experiences**

Dr. Melissa A. Louvar Reeves

**DEPRESSION
Signs and Strategies for
Counselors,
Educators, and Parents**

Dr. Melisa Marsh

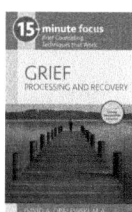

**GRIEF
Processing and Recovery**

David A. Opalewski, M.A.

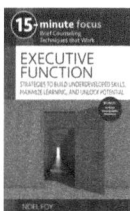

**EXECUTIVE FUNCTION
Strategies To Build
Underdeveloped Skills, Maximize
Learning, and Unlock Potential**

Noel Foy

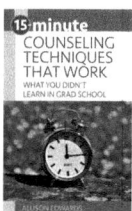

**15-MINUTE COUNSELING
TECHNIQUES THAT WORK
What You Didn't Learn
in Grad School**

Allison Edwards

NATIONAL CENTER for
YOUTH ISSUES

About NCYI

National Center for Youth Issues provides educational resources, training, and support programs to foster the healthy social, emotional, and physical development of children and youth. Since our founding in 1981, NCYI has established a reputation as one of the country's leading providers of teaching materials and training for counseling and student-support professionals. NCYI helps meet the immediate needs of students throughout the nation by ensuring those who mentor them are well prepared to respond across the developmental spectrum.

Connect With Us Online!

@nationalcenterforyouthissues

@ncyi

@nationalcenterforyouthissues